B₁

Past-into-Present Series

RELIGION

Hugh Bodey

Director, Colne Valley Museum, Yorkshire

B. T. BATSFORD LTD London

First published 1973
© Hugh Bodey, 1973

Printed in Great Britain by
Redwood Press Ltd., Trowbridge, Wiltshire
for the publishers
B. T. Batsford Ltd, 4 Fitzhardinge Street, London W1H 0AH
ISBN 0 7134 1786 2

To my Mother

Acknowledgments

The Author is grateful for much time and advice given to him by the Reverend and Mrs R. J. Sleigh.

The Author and Publisher would like to thank the following for the illustrations which appear in this book: Aerofilms for fig. 25; the Ashmolean Museum for fig. 3; the Bibliothèque Nationale, Paris for fig. 27; H. A. Bodey for fig. 63; P. T. Bodey for figs 12, 23; Cirencester Museum for fig. 8; the British Museum for figs 9, 10, 34, 41; the Courtauld Institute for fig. 24; the Department of the Environment (Crown copyright) for fig. 26; Gloucester City Museums for fig. 38; the *Huddersfield Examiner* for figs 1, 15, 29, 65; Hull City Museums for fig. 43; Dr J. K. St Joseph for fig. 2; the London Museum for figs 6, 7; the Mansell Collection for fig. 58; the National Building Record for fig. 59; Redland Park Church, Bristol for fig. 62; the Sutcliffe Gallery for fig. 56; Taylor Woodrow for fig. 64; the Victoria and Albert Museum (Crown copyright) for fig. 47. They also wish to thank R. J. Whittaker who drew the maps; Penguin Books Ltd for permission to reprint the extract from *Beowulf*, translated by David Wright (Penguin Classic, 1957), and Basil Blackwell Ltd and Dr W. O. Hassall for the quotation on page 43, which appeared in *They Saw It Happen 55 BC–1485* by Hassal and Hales.

Contents

The Illustrations

1 Druids, Romans and Christians

Religion is the hardest subject to write about, and many people even find it embarrassing to discuss. This may partly be because it has to do with the unknown, with death and what happens after that; the unknown is always frightening. Religion can also be a dull affair, tinged with sadness, which would be enough to put anyone off.

Religion is one of the oldest matters that has ever been explored. We all seem to have a natural desire to worship something greater than ourselves, and this need is the beginning of religion. It involves everyone to some extent and, so far as Britain is concerned, has shaped and moulded the way we live now. Similarly, what we believe now, and the way we live because of what we believe, will affect the people that come after us.

Religion is complicated still further because the way people behave is based on it. The morals of a person or a country are based on what the person or country believes. If, for example, people believe that life is precious and that there is some

1 Woodhenge, Wiltshire. The plan indicates the shape of this typical henge but its religious function is not known. Sun-worship may have been the basis of ceremonies

reason for living (religion), they will look on murder and other forms of killing as wrong (morals). A person's morals guide the way he lives; a country's morals lead to laws being passed to encourage everyone in the country to follow the same rules. A discussion of religion, therefore, inevitably includes some mention of morals, which are an off-shoot of religion.

Religion has often brought out the best in people. For example, in the middle ages some of the best architects were employed in building Christian cathedrals, because it was felt that only the best was good enough for God. In the nineteenth century Elizabeth Fry accepted much ridicule and abuse because her religion led her to help the women in the appalling prison conditions of that time. Religion has also been the source of much bitterness between rival groups, to the credit of none.

Perhaps these opening paragraphs have set out some of the difficulties involved in studying religion in Britain over the past 2,000 years. Further difficulties will become apparent. One is the different shades of meaning attached to the words which are used to talk about religion. The word 'church' is an example, and its many meanings will become clearer in the following chapter.

Before the Druids

The beginnings of religion seem as old as men in the world. Just about every tribe at every stage in the world's history has had a religion of some kind. Many tribes have worshipped the sun and with good reason. The sun provided warmth that made life more comfortable, it controlled the seasons and made plants grow and above all it was reliable—it came every day without fail and set the pattern for daily life.

It may well be that the earliest religion practised in Britain was worship of the sun. Ancient structures like Stonehenge on Salisbury Plain seem to have much to do with the position of the sun at particular moments, and the position of other planets and stars. In recent years much research has been carried out on these monuments (and there are many of them in Britain and other European countries)

2 Some henges were small. This one at Arbor Low, Derbyshire, has only one circle of stones, surrounded by a ditch and wall. The number of these circles is an indication of their importance to people

and it is beginning to look as if the people who built them had a considerable understanding of the movements of the sun, moon and stars. The information mattered to them because they were farmers. They had to have some way of determining when to sow seeds. It is likely that religious practices were connected with the study of the universe, but of what kind can be little more than guess-work.

Celtic Life and Religion

Coming nearer our own day, the picture becomes a little clearer, though there is much that is not known even of events 2,000 years ago. Britain and its inhabitants at that time were very different from now. In the first place, the land was mostly covered with thick forest. Wild animals were in their element and greatly outnumbered and terrified the small number of people living in Britain. The population at this time can be little more than speculation but a total of one million for the whole of Britain is probably a generous estimate. Most of the people lived in the main river valleys of southern England, such as the Thames and Severn, where the climate and soil made the growing of crops possible. The people lived in small villages, made up of circular huts with thatched roofs. Some villages kept animals like pigs and sheep, and others were hunted in the surrounding forest to add to the larder.

The villages were separate from each other and were constantly afraid of being attacked. The villagers belonged to one or other of the main tribes inhabiting Britain at that time, which frequently fought among themselves. Belonging to a village, however, was more important than membership of a tribe.

Britain was thus fragmented into a large number of small communities for most of the time; only if danger threatened did they think of themselves as belonging to a tribe. Their religion was just as fragmented, which has made it difficult for the archaeologists to piece together. No gods were respected by all the Celtic tribes; indeed forty gods and goddesses are known to have been worshipped and there may well have been others. Some of the gods were linked with a particular place. Sulis was revered as the goddess of the hot springs at Bath in Somerset, but was hardly known elsewhere. The goddess Brigantia, on the other hand, was honoured throughout the Brigantes tribe, in an area from the South Pennines to the Tyne. Other gods were associated with particular activities, such as Nodens the hunter, to whom a large temple was built at Lydney in Gloucestershire.

What ceremonies were conducted in this and other temples is a mystery. We may imagine that every temple had its priest or priestess, and that the worshippers made gifts of food or manufactured objects. A worshipper at the temple of Nodens may well have gone in before a hunt and asked for success, and returned later with part of the kill if he had been successful. There are, however, no records of what happened before the Romans came, though there is considerable information then, for the Romans brought their own religious habits and added them to what they found.

7

3 An Iron Age hill fort at Uffington Castle in Berkshire has a horse carved in the chalk beside it. The horse, also cut in the Iron Age, may have had connections with religious customs

Druids

One religious group the Romans could not tolerate was the Druids. They had met them before Julius Caesar made his raid on Britain in 55 BC, for the Druids were also strong in Gaul (now France) and in other countries of western Europe. This was one of the reasons the Romans disliked them—the Druids had organised links in the Roman Empire and beyond. The Romans' main opposition was based on the human sacrifices made by the Druids, a practice that revolted Roman feelings, since they had suppressed such sacrifices within the empire a century before. Their writings condemn the Druids for these habits, but give little information about what else they did.

It would seem that their worship was closely connected with nature. Ceremonies were conducted in forest clearings away from villages. An oak tree with mistletoe growing in it, a rare sight, was regarded as sacred and therefore a suitable ceremonial site. A Roman writer called Pliny watched such a ceremony, which was held on the sixth day of the moon. (Many ancient people calculated events according to the phases of the moon. Their 'day' started with the night when the moon could be seen and was followed by daylight, whereas our day ends with the night. The moon's phases, spread over twenty-eight days, made a convenient way of fixing a date, and were more easily recognised than the phases of the sun. The Druids had a full calendar relating the activities of the sun and moon spread over nineteen years, which equalled 235 lunar months.) Pliny watched as a Druid, dressed in a white robe, climbed the oak and cut a branch of mistletoe with a golden sickle, and the falling branch was caught on a white cloak. Two white bulls were then sacrificed, and perhaps searched for good or bad omens. The ceremony was followed by a feast.

The Druids were also responsible for preserving laws and customs, which were memorised in verse form. The training of the priests took a very long time, some records say nineteen years. They held high rank in each tribe, and were respected as holy men. They were not expected to take part in battles, and advised in legal disputes. People living at the time thought that the priests understood the wishes of the gods, and treated them with great respect. For this reason, Druids were able to travel in safety from one tribe to another, both in Britain and other countries. This may have been another reason for Roman dislike, for a network of mobile and respected men could soon whip up rebellion. There is no evidence that this ever happened, but it must have seemed a possibility. Certainly the Druids were the only people, religious or otherwise, who could have united the Celts against the Roman invaders. For whatever reasons, the Romans crushed the Druids during the middle years of the first century AD and left only a few shut up in their headquarters on Anglesey.

Roman Customs

In their place, the Romans brought many religious practices of their own when the full conquest of Britain began in AD 43. The first to be established was worship of the emperor, a practice common in the rest of the empire. An extravagant temple was built in Colchester for emperor-worship with a large court, a great altar and niches for many statues. The priestly duties were shared between ten tribes, who also had to organise and pay for the festivals and athletics matches connected with the temple. It was burnt down in AD 61 during a revolt led by queen Boudicca and probably moved to London. A temple to the family of the emperor was built in all the larger towns. The worship was conducted by six priests who were drawn, by law, from among the wealthy traders. They needed to be wealthy, because they not only had to pay for any festivals they might organise, but also for the costs of mending bridges and streets and installing sewers.

9

Worship of the emperor was important as a sign of loyalty from a conquered people. It also helped to unite and pacify the many tribes and link them with others in the empire. Emperor-worship was often linked with the worship of other Roman gods. The blacksmiths' gild in Chichester dedicated a temple to Neptune and Minerva 'for the welfare of the Divine House', by which they meant the family of the emperor. Despite Boudicca's rebellion, emperor-worship became accepted as a normal part of religious life among Roman citizens. It was, however, very much an official religion, observed by Roman officials and sympathisers as the thing to do. It meant nothing to the rest of the population.

Worship of the Roman gods also meant little to the natives of Britain. Chief among them was Jupiter Optimus Maximus, to whom more temples and altars were dedicated than any of the others. Worship of Jupiter was the official religion in the army, and was carried out by the regiment's commandant in the presence

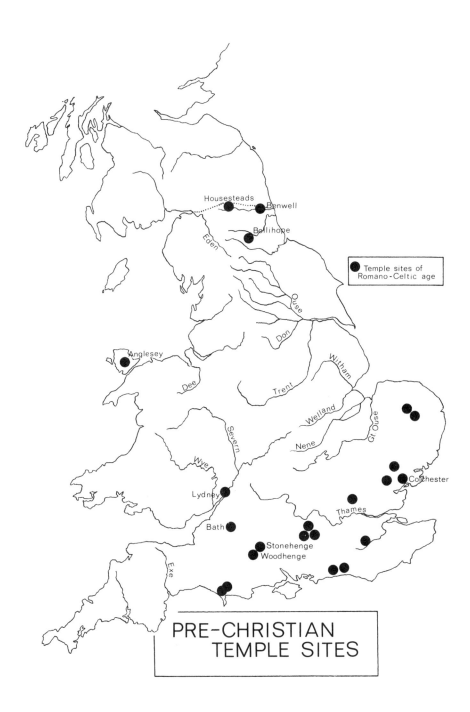

Housesteads • •Benwell

Bollihope

● Temple sites of
Romano-Celtic age

•Anglesey

•Lydney

Colchester

Bath•

•Stonehenge
•Woodhenge

PRE-CHRISTIAN
TEMPLE SITES

5 Pre-Christian temple sites. The named sites are explained more fully in the text, the others
are temple sites as indicated. These are known largely as a result of archaeological investigations

6 An artist's impression, based on excavations, of the temple to Mithras at Walbrook on the Thames. The apse can be clearly seen, and note also the lack of windows

of the troops drawn up to witness the ceremony. New altars were put up each year to Jupiter and the old ones reverently buried. The commandant took vows for the welfare of the state on 1 January, and for the safety of the empire and emperor on 3 January each year.

This official religion did not appeal to the troops much, who chose their own gods. Mars, the god of war, meant more to a soldier, as it did to many Celts who had a similar god under different names. Foreign troops often brought the worship of their own gods, such as the Syrian archers who worshipped the goddess Hammia at Carvoran, or the Frisii from central Europe who had a temple to Mars Thincsus at Housesteads on Hadrian's Wall. Most buildings in a fortress had a presiding god, such as Epona, the goddess of ostlers, who ruled the stable block. The longer the conquest lasted (the last troops left in 410) the more mixing there was between Roman and Celtic gods, and many temples included the worship of several of each. On the whole, the troops preferred to worship Celtic gods rather than their own, and there was much compromise. A Roman soldier called Gaius built a shrine in the third century on the wild moors of Bollihope in the Wear valley. The shrine was dedicated to the god Silvanus Invictus, and Gaius gave thanks 'after catching a lovely boar which previous hunters had hunted in vain'.

The temples used for worship looked alike. The central part was a high, square sanctuary, the holy place that was the god's home. It was lit by windows near the roof. Around the outside of the sanctuary was a large square veranda. The temple was not meant to hold many people; these could come with their offerings a few at a time, or larger numbers could be addressed from the veranda. There were no sit-down services for large congregations. This kind of temple had been built by the Celts before the Romans came. The Romans' knowledge of new building materials and methods led to larger temples being built, and the Romans also adorned the temples with carvings and paintings. Some Roman temples had a semi-circular extension on one side called an apse. A temple at Benwell on Hadrian's Wall had a statue in the apse, and an altar on each side to the two gods of the temple.

Most of the gods honoured by the Romans came from western Europe. A few from eastern countries were also worshipped in Britain, though often only for short intervals. The western gods were normally worshipped by one person representing many others, such as the commandant taking vows for the regiment. The eastern religions expected a more personal involvement. In the temples of Jupiter Dolichenus, a priest interpreted the god's orders and advice to individuals who came with problems. The most highly organised of these cults was of the Persian god, Mithras. High standards of conduct and honesty were expected from his followers, who were mostly army officers and successful merchants. The churches seldom held more than a dozen: the cult called for too much mental and spiritual effort when the alternative gods required very little.

There was, then, a very great variety in the religious life of the province under the Romans, who accepted all gods as being suitable to worship and linked them with their own. In this way they tried to show toleration for the gods of conquered tribes and at the same time teach them Roman customs. In this they were successful and slowly made Britons more aware of belonging to a large empire. Such a

7 A carved plaque showing Mithras killing a bull. The plaque came from a temple built in the second century

13

world-wide empire really called for a world-wide religion — even the Romans ceased to take emperor-worship seriously. Part of the success of Christianity was that it was a world-wide religion, far beyond any local shrines.

Christianity in Britain

How Christianity first came to Britain is quite unknown. Many legends grew up in later centuries to explain its arrival, and one of the most charming ones is that Joseph of Arimathea crossed to Britain and built a wattle church at Glastonbury. There are very few facts, however. Early in the third century, parts of Britain that had not been conquered by the Romans were Christian. It seems fair to think that Christianity came to this country at some time in the second century, and it is probable that Christian traders were largely responsible, or perhaps Christian troops. It is even possible that people escaped to Britain from Rome, where intense and savage persecution raged under many emperors until 260. Christianity was a semi-secret organisation because of the persecution. The Emperor Diocletian ordered a purge of Christians early in the fourth century; many churches were destroyed and the first English Christians were martyred. The best known of these is St Alban.

Very soon after this persecution, the churches were rebuilt and the British church was sufficiently large and organised to send representatives to conferences arranged by the whole Christian Church. (For the rest of this book, Church will mean all the Christians of every denomination; church will mean either a denomination within the Church or a building.) These conferences were encouraged by the emperor Constantine (312–337) who was declared emperor in York. He promised to tolerate all religions by the Edict of Milan in 313, but in fact robbed the funds of pagan temples to build Christian churches. He also made Sunday a day when no unnecessary work was to be done. The Bishops of York and London were two of the three from Britain who travelled to the Council of Arles in 314, and others attended other conferences at intervals in the fourth century. It seems likely that most Christians were found among the poor in the towns and in the highlands, but that few among the wealthy villa owners wished to be associated with the new religion. Apart from what may have been a fourth century church in Silchester, very few remains of Christian activities have been found, so that the picture is incomplete. It seems likely that Christianity was still only a minority religion at this time, and several of the Celtic cults experienced a revival at the end of the fourth century. The temple to Nodens at Lydney was popular at this time.

Things had changed somewhat by 400. Calpurnius, father of St Patrick, was a landowner and member of the governing class in the Bristol Channel area. He was also a deacon in the local church. Every large town had its bishop by this time, who took services in the only church in the town and taught new members. (He was not responsible for a large area, as bishops later became.) He was the only person who had any training, and probably very little of it, and deacons were

```
ROTAS
OPERA
TENET
AREPO
SATOR
```

8 These letters scratched in the plaster of a Roman house in Gloucestershire are evidence of Christians in Britain. The letters can be read forwards or backwards. They mean little by themselves but can be re-arranged to read *Pater Noster* (Our Father)

selected from among the congregation to help in running the church. If Calpurnius was a good example of other landowners, then the wealthier members of society were accepting Christian ways, at least in the towns. The old ways were still firmly held in country areas, where most of the population lived, and Christianity did not triumph there until 500 or even later. Gildas wrote of west Britain in the middle of the sixth century that 'before the coming of Christ [to these people] divine honours had been heaped by a populace, blind as it then was, upon mountains and hills and rivers'. It would seem from this as if many of the shrines at waterfalls and other sacred sites had been abandoned in favour of Christianity.

The Church was mainly organised in the towns. The first monastery was set up in 397 by a man called Ninian. He had been educated in Rome and, when he returned to Britain, he set up the monastery at Whithorn in Galloway. Monks and priests trained there blazed a trail along Hadrian's Wall to the Tyne and southwards into Yorkshire, a route followed later by Irish missionaries.

Christianity probably spread to Ireland in the fourth century, certainly before St Patrick was made bishop and sent to work there in 432. At much the same time St Illtud began to preach in Wales, and later taught St David. Close links were kept between the churches in Britain, Gaul and Italy, so the Church was united and followed similar customs. The method of fixing the date of Easter, for example, was agreed at the Council of Arles in 314, and all the churches did the same. The method was modified in 455, and all the churches accepted the change. The links between churches in Britain and Italy were broken shortly afterwards, when the Roman Empire began to split apart.

2   Christianity Spreads

From the middle of the fourth century the Roman Empire began to collapse under attacks from the barbarian tribes of Europe. Garrisons on the Saxon shore, stretching from Brancaster in Norfolk to Porchester in Hampshire, had to repel Saxon invaders and the troops succeeded only as long as the garrisons were kept up to full strength. As more troops were recalled to defend Rome itself, and particularly when the last left in 410, the invaders found little resistance. The Britons had given up rebelling against Roman rule in south-east England long before, and had looked to the Romans for protection. They were no match for the boat-loads of determined Saxons, Angles and Jutes that fell on the unprotected coast, and settled there from the mid-fifth century onwards. The Britons were forced to abandon the towns and were swept back into the hilly regions of Cornwall, Wales and the north of England, while the new-comers from what are now Denmark and north Germany took the lower agricultural areas.

Saxon Religion

The Church was almost crushed out of existence in the areas conquered by the invaders. Many churches were destroyed and valuables stolen as the Britons fled westwards, taking their religion with them and leaving few Christians behind. However, judging by the speed with which Christianity sprang up later in some of the eastern areas, some Christians may have stayed loyal to their religion and even impressed the invaders; but for many years the new-comers clung to their own religion.

Little is known of this, for the few Anglo-Saxon books that have survived mostly date from a later time when Christianity had been accepted by them. It seems likely that many gods were worshipped, in common with the peoples left in Germany. Only four are known by name and these are all remembered in the names of the middle days of the week. They are Tiw, Woden, Thunor and Frig. Woden was worshipped the most widely of these, and his name is remembered in Woodnesborough near Sandwich in Kent, in Wednesbury and Wednesfield in Staffordshire and in Wansdyke (Woden's dyke) at Pewsey in Wiltshire. Kings claimed to be descended from Woden but ordinary men also worshipped him as the maker of anything unusual. Thunor, the thunder-god, was honoured among all the Jute and Saxon tribes, as at Thursley in Surrey and Thundersley in Essex. Tiw was the god of war, and is known to have been worshipped in the Vale of the Red Horse in south Warwickshire. No sites are known of the goddess Frig, and

9 The Bible had to be copied out by hand, and each copy was treated with great respect. The beginnings of chapters were richly ornamented, as in this page of the Lindisfarne Gospels. These were made in the 720s, and the patterns are typical of Celtic art

nothing is known of how these gods were worshipped. It seems that the Saxon new year started on 25 December, that there was a celebration of the return of spring connected with a goddess called Eostre and that the eighth month of the year was called 'the month of offerings', which suggests some kind of harvest festival. Saxons believed that their lives were controlled by fate—what was going to happen would happen. Connected with this rather gloomy thought was a feeling that the only thing a man could have for the future was fame: let a man therefore behave bravely and not break the law. There was nothing to live for, and nothing to die for either. Some people in Britain still accept these views.

Growth of the Celtic Church

There may have been more to Saxon religion than is yet known. Certainly it had a firm hold on the various tribes in the sixth century, and any attempts to introduce Christianity to the Saxon settlers were markedly unsuccessful. It is probable that no such attempts were made by the Britons. They would have had little desire to face again the people who had chased them from their homes with violence.

The invasion must also have made a considerable difference to the Celtic church. As has been seen, this largely grew in the towns of Roman Britain. The Saxon invasions forced the Celts to return to their tribal hill-forts and the pattern of bishops guiding Christians in the towns was no longer possible. Instead, the Celtic church developed in two ways. Christians now met in their tribes, and the bishops led groups of people. Many monasteries also were founded, both for men and women, particularly in Wales in the sixth century, many of them under the

17

imago leonis

OAGI
HM
R

US
CUS

10 The Lindisfarne Gospels were made on Holy Island off the Northumberland coast. They include full-page pictures of the four Gospel writers, more typical of Roman art. This is St Mark

guidance of St David. That century also saw many of the most illustrious of saints. (The early Church used 'saint' as a word of respect for people who displayed some of the characteristics of Christ, or who helped other people to know Christ. Their example was worth copying.) The Celtic monasteries were small and simple places. Unlike the graceful buildings of a later age, these had wattle and daub walls and a rough thatch. Conditions were harsh, as was intended. It helped to keep the attention of the monks and nuns on their prayers and study of the Bible and lives of the saints. It was common for the monks to use such monasteries as bases from which to set out to teach local villages or as missionaries in new areas.

The Celtic Christians kept in close touch with one another. The sea was no barrier to them and coracles were used between Cornwall, Wales and Ireland. Links with the rest of the Church were broken, however, by the solid Saxon settlements barring the way to Rome. The decisions of the Roman church after 450 did not reach the Celtic church, which continued in the way it had always done things. This inability to learn of changes in the rest of Europe was to cause problems later.

The Celtic church seems to have decided that it had enough to do in its own area without seeking to extend its influence outside. This was very probably the case since most Christians had been the poor, living in towns up to the time the Romans left Britain. Most people lived outside the towns and had little contact with Christian teaching; the word 'pagan' meant both a non-Christian and someone living in the country. The end of town-living may have presented a great deal of work for the fifth-century Christians, with new people to teach about Christ and many churches to build.

Not until the mid-sixth century is there any sign of missionary activity. An Irish prince sailed to Scotland in 563 and set up a monastery on the island of Iona. This soon served as a base from which to send preachers among the Scots. No attempts seem to have been made at this time to send missionaries among the Saxons, neither did any come from Brittany or other parts of France.

Augustine's Mission

The first attempt to convert the Saxons was organised by Pope Gregory in Rome. It had long been his wish to go in person to Britain; being pope prevented him but gave him the power to send someone else. He chose a man called Augustine and sent him off on the hazardous journey through France to a country known to be wild and dangerous. Augustine tried to get out of it, but Gregory was firm. After a journey taking over a year, Augustine and forty monks landed in Kent on the island of Thanet in 597. They knew already that Bertha, wife of the King of Kent, was a Christian, but they also knew that she had not been able to persuade the king to take any interest in her religion. King Ethelbert met Augustine in the open air, afraid of what might happen to him. He soon became convinced at least of their honesty, and gave them a house in Canterbury, food and permission

11 The head of a stone cross found in Crofthorne. This design is also Celtic in style

to preach to anyone who would listen. On the east of the town was an old church which they repaired and made into a monastery — they had gained a foothold in one of the British kingdoms. 25 December had already been adopted as Christmas Day in other parts of Europe, and fitted in with the local custom.

Ethelbert was converted in time, and many of his nobles also. This encouraged Augustine to set about restoring the old churches in Kent and some new ones were built. He was made Bishop of the Church in Britain, with the responsibility of instructing and correcting other British bishops. It was his intention to move the centre of the Church to London as soon as he could, and to divide southern England into twelve areas with a bishop in charge of each. (In fact this was not achieved until 737.) He also intended to have a similar system in the north, based on York. (The first bishop of the Roman church was appointed to York in 735, and there were only three bishops under him by the ninth century.) In these ways, Augustine laid the basis of Christianity in England again, and on different lines from the way the Celtic church had run itself. Bishops in the Roman church were in charge of a large area, called a diocese, and the bishop was responsible for the training of priests, the good management of churches and monasteries and the religion of all the people. He confirmed new members into the Church but otherwise there was much less personal contact between bishop and people than there was in the Celtic church.

There were other differences too between the Celtic and Roman churches, and Augustine tried to solve the differences by meeting the Celtic bishops. He did not make it too obvious that he had been put in charge of all bishops in Britain but even so no agreement could be found. The main stumbling block was the method used to work out the date of Easter each year (based on the phases of the moon). The Celtic church used the formula agreed before the arrival of the Saxons. Some changes had been made since that time which put the Celtic church out of step with the rest of the Church. The Celtic bishops showed no liking for the new-comers, and the strict but simple kind of religion of the Celts had nothing to gain from the more elaborate Roman church. The two sides therefore went their separate ways.

The Roman church in Kent soon had its own problems. Ethelbert died in 616 and the new king was less interested in Christianity. The church nearly collapsed without royal protection but managed to keep going until the new king was also converted, and his son went so far as to order the destruction of all the old idols in Kent. Reaction against Christianity among the East Saxons was even stronger, and the church named after St Paul in London, founded in 601, was abandoned for forty years. Slowly the Church in south-east England made headway, providing places for education and worship. The setbacks were discouraging but not permanent. By contrast, when Paulinus travelled north and made a rapid conversion of Northumbria, he went too fast and left no way of training the new Christians. Consequently the new religion was easily overthrown in 732 and Northumbria returned to the gods it knew.

12 The Vikings from Denmark and Norway included Christians. They had their own ideas on what was artistic, which are reflected in this stone coffin, to be seen at Burnsall in Yorkshire

Missionary Activities

The differences between the Celtic and Roman customs did not prevent them from continuing side by side. An example of this was the conversion of East Anglia in the mid-seventh century. Felix was sent as bishop from Kent, and was given land at Dunwich for a church. He soon started a school as well, and sent to Kent for teachers. Fursa arrived at much the same time from Ireland, and started a monastery in a deserted fort, probably at Burgh in Suffolk. There was no conflict between the two groups of Christians. Instead, they became a well-knit community and survived many bad times until Danish invaders conquered East Anglia and overwhelmed them all.

Christianity was restored to Northumbria by monks from Iona, led by Aidan. He was invited to come in 634 by King Oswald, who had been educated in a Celtic monastery. Aidan settled on the island of Lindisfarne (now more often called Holy Island) and established a monastery. Aidan was the bishop for Northumbria but was quite indifferent to the dignity the Roman church expected to give a bishop. The monastery was bleak, and had no church until Aidan's successor built one of timber and thatch. Yet Aidan was well-known and liked by people in the north, and greatly respected by church leaders in the south. He tried to show by the example of his own life how Christians should behave, rather than attaching importance to arguments over the date of Easter and similar petty differences. Many nobles gave him land for churches and monasteries. The most famous of the ones founded at this time was the Abbey at Whitby, of which the Abbess Hilda was the first and most respected leader. Missionaries also went from Lindisfarne to preach in Mercia, Middle Anglia, Lindsey and Essex.

Christianity in Britain had thus taken a firm hold within two generations of Augustine landing in Kent. Offshoots of the two churches were to be found in all

THE KINGDOMS
OF ENGLAND c 800.

Iona

STRATH-
CLYDE

Lindisfarne

GALLOWAY

Whithorn

NORTHUMBRIA

Whitby

Man

Ripon

York

Humber

Anglesey

LINDSEY

Offas Dyke

EAST
ANGLIA

MERCIA

MIDDLE
ANGLIA

Dunwich

WELSH
KINGDOMS

ESSEX

London

Thames

Thanet
Canterbury

Severn

KENT

WESSEX

SUSSEX

WEST
WALES

Wight

13 The kingdoms of England. Britain was fragmented into many kingdoms in the ninth century, each separate from the others. Christianity was the only religion to be found in all the kingdoms. (Places marked are mentioned in the text)

parts of the country, which made it more necessary than ever to settle the differences between the two. As has too often happened in religious history, the two sides agreed completely on everything that mattered but disagreed over details of ceremony and organisation. Often, members of any religion cling to old beliefs and customs just because they are traditional, without really examining the meaning behind them. To settle the differences, Abbess Hilda called a council of both sides to meet at Whitby in 663, and a decision was made to follow Roman customs. It was now possible to unite the church in Britain under one leader, the Archbishop of Canterbury. A few Celtic Christians returned to Ireland but the majority stayed where they were and gradually adopted the new ways. As a result, Christianity in Britain has always been a mixture of the two traditions. The colourful ritual to be found in many churches and the eye-catching architecture and ornament of the Roman church is matched by the full involvement of the congregation in singing, in leading services and in studying the Bible, the characteristics of the Celtic church. By 633, there was a bishop in every kingdom except Sussex and Christianity was the dominant religion. The old religions were still being followed in many parts, though often in secret.

Church Organisation

The church was able to grow steadily and in peace for the next century and more. Theodore became Archbishop of Canterbury in 669 and established a pattern of organisation that was to be followed for many centuries. This was the division of dioceses into parishes, with a parish priest responsible for all the people in his area. Parishes were made by consultation with the kings and nobles who governed Britain, and it took several generations before the inhabited parts of Britain were divided into parishes. With it came the necessity of collecting contributions from the people in a parish towards the payment of the priest. Slowly it became normal

14 Masonry from derelict Roman buildings was used to erect the church at Escombe in Co Durham. It was built between 700 and 750. The chancel (where the altar is) is ten feet (about 3 metres) square

for a tithe of some of the farm produce to be given to the priest (a tithe was a tenth). The goods collected in this way were to be used to feed the priest, and also to be given by him to pilgrims and the poor. There are signs that, at this time, the tithes were used for these purposes and to some extent operated as a simple insurance system against starvation.

Many parishes at first had no parish church. Services were held in the open air, and a cross set up to mark the site. People would gather from the surrounding countryside and a priest would meet them, to pray and read the Bible. Many such ancient crosses still stand in places where no church was ever built, others were later absorbed into a church.

Importance of Monasteries

Monasteries continued to be popular in the seventh and eighth centuries, and new ones were founded following both Celtic and Roman customs. There were many motives behind founding a monastery. One founder was Guthlac, who was descended from a family of kings and was expected to spend his life fighting, as all his family had. Being a young man, he thought this was a waste of his life and instead built himself a shelter in the fens of Middle Anglia and spent his life in prayer and study. Others gathered round to learn from him as the years passed, and the house gradually became the centre of Crowland Abbey. In Northumbria, an earl built a small monastery at the mouth of the Humber and became its leader. The life of prayer, study and preaching to others seemed exciting and important to all kinds of people at this time, and the monasteries were lively places. Anyone could ask to join a monastery—they did not have to be rich or well educated, just enthusiastic. There were many different kinds of monastery for the founder of each one felt he could choose the rules by which it was to be run. Some families made their homes into monasteries and followed a daily pattern of prayer and study. It was more usual for someone with the necessary land or money to found a monastery and invite a neighbouring monastery to send a few monks to set the pattern. This soon attracted other people to join. Often these were independent and ran themselves; others were in federations where the abbot of the oldest monastery set the rules for all the others and controlled them. The Abbot of Medeshamstede (Peterborough) controlled monasteries in Leicestershire, Surrey, Kent and Northamptonshire, where he had been asked to send monks to start new monasteries. There were some double houses, where monks and nuns had buildings side by side. All these houses were governed by women. At Wimborne in Dorset, the two communities had their own buildings, even separate churches, and the abbess gave her orders to the monks through a window. Other double houses often shared the church and held joint services. Most of these were swept away by the Danish invasions of the ninth century, and the survivors were regarded as unfashionable in the tenth. By that time, increasing numbers of monasteries were following the rules laid down by St Benedict in 529 for his Italian monastery.

15 This cross dates from the fifteenth century, and is at Ampney Crucis in Gloucestershire. There may have been an earlier preaching cross on the same site

The Church in Britain was sufficiently strong to be able to send out missionaries. Willibrord went off to Frisia at the end of the seventh century and Boniface to Germany in the eighth. Both these and others left their mark on the lands they visited. Clearly also they came from a predominantly Christian country that they could draw on for support. Contemporary writings confirm the view that Britain was basically Christian. The unknown author of the poem *Beowulf* was a Christian, and writing for a Christian audience, though the subject of the poem was a mixture of myth and pre-Christian practices. It is a tale of the conflict of good and evil and, while the underlying tone is Christian, the people and their actions are largely pagan. Two quotations may illustrate the contrast.

With this the hero laid his cheek against the pillow. Around him many brave seafarers sank to rest in the hall. Not one supposed that he would ever leave it to revisit his native land, his family, or the town where he grew up; for they knew that in the past slaughter had carried off far too many of the Danes in that banqueting hall. But God gave the luck of battle to the Geats. He furnished them with help, so that they all overcame their enemy through the skill and strength of one man. It is sure that almighty God has always ruled over human race.

The old customs did not need to be explained but could be taken for granted among his hearers. The hero had died famous and was given an appropriate funeral:

> Upon the headland the Geats erected a broad high tumulus, plainly visible to distant seamen. In ten days they completed the building of the Hero's beacon. Round his ashes they built the finest vault that their most skilful men could devise. Within the barrow they placed collars, brooches and all the trappings. . .

The old religion may still have been practised in secret even in the eighth century.

The century of steady growth in the Church came to an abrupt end with the main Danish invasion in 865. Scattered raids by Vikings from Norway had begun in 786 and caused havoc enough with churches being robbed, villages burnt and people enslaved, but they had been isolated attacks. The Danish invasion was to capture and colonise land; East Anglia, the eastern half of Mercia and south Northumbria were taken. Monastic life was destroyed in eastern England and church organisation was shattered. The bishoprics of Dunwich, Elmham and Lindsey were blotted out, and many others became unworkable. Lindisfarne was abandoned and its bishop travelled from one place to another for seven years until a new cathedral could be built at Chester-le-Street.

The first shock was the worst. The Danes soon settled down in their new country and were not violently anti-Christian. Indeed the first king of Danish Northumbria, Guthfrith, was Christian, though the others were not. In time the age-old practice of sending missionaries into eastern England began again, and slowly the people began to adopt Christian ways. The British Church had been severely strained and disorganised, though, and it was not until the tenth century that it pulled itself together.

3 One Church

Monasteries were the core of the Church for the thousand years from 500. St Benedict had set a pattern in Italy in 529, and this had been followed in most monasteries throughout Europe, as was seen in the previous chapter. People looked on the monastic way of life for most of the thousand years as the proper and natural way to be a Christian. People from every possible kind of background cheerfully left their homes and, if they had any, their possessions, in preference for a life of prayer, reading of the Bible and lives of the saints and hard work. There were very many monastery buildings so that few people lived far from a monastery. In this and other ways, monasteries had considerable influence over those living outside them. Nowadays the reverse is true, and few of us live near an active monastery; indeed, you may not know where the nearest is. We tend to think that the life of the monastery is outdated or even that it failed as long ago as the fifteenth century. It is hard for us to imagine a time when it went without saying that to spend your life as a nun or monk was both the best and the most natural thing to do.

If we can imagine that way of thinking, it makes it easier to understand the ups and downs of the tenth to the fifteenth century.

16 The 70-foot (21-metre) tower of this church is Saxon. The church is at Earls Barton in Northamptonshire, and the tower was built about 980

Reform in the Tenth Century

Most of the monasteries had declined by the beginning of the tenth century, as they had in other parts of Europe. The reasons for this decline were a mixture of many factors. Undoubtedly some of the monasteries had grown too wealthy, which allowed the monks too easy a life, and they neglected their duties. There was little contact between one monastery and another, except in the federations mentioned in the eighth century. It often happened that when the founder of a monastery grew old, no one else had the same enthusiasm and there was no central person to turn to for guidance. It seems that many monasteries lasted a generation or two and then faded away. A drastic cause of decay amongst them was the Danish settlement, and the fighting and destruction associated with it.

For these reasons there were hardly any monasteries left when Alfred became king of Wessex in 871. He wished to see a revival of the monasteries, but had to invite foreign monks when he founded one at Athelney. A nunnery at Shaftesbury in Wiltshire was more successful, and a number of other nunneries followed soon after. The important role of women in this revival is notable.

17 The church at Greenstead, Chipping Ongar, Essex. It has been much adapted over the years but the walls of split oak logs are part of the original Saxon church

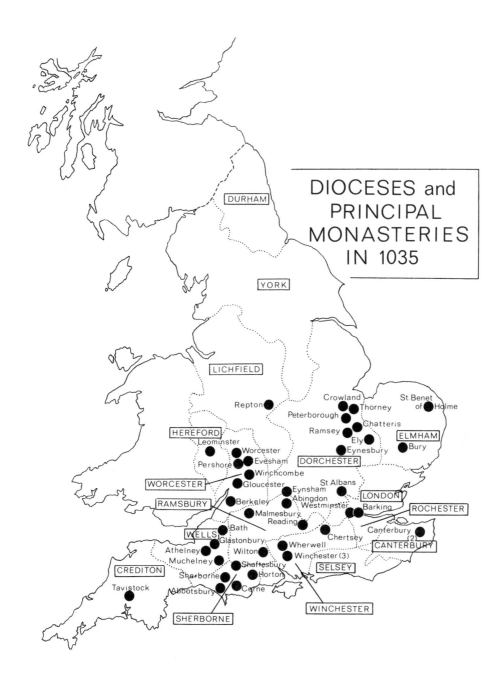

DIOCESES and PRINCIPAL MONASTERIES IN 1035

DURHAM

YORK

LICHFIELD

Repton

Crowland
Thorney
St.Benet of Holme
Peterborough
Chatteris
Ramsey
ELMHAM
Ely
Bury
Eynesbury

HEREFORD
Leominster
Worcester
Evesham
DORCHESTER
Pershore
Winchcombe
WORCESTER
Gloucester
St Albans
Eynsham
Berkeley
Abingdon
LONDON
RAMSBURY
Westminster
Barking
ROCHESTER
Malmesbury
Reading
WELLS
Bath
Canterbury (2)
Athelney
Glastonbury
Wherwell
Chertsey
CANTERBURY
Muchelney
Wilton
Winchester (3)
CREDITON
Shaftesbury
SELSEY
Tavistock
Sherborne
Horton
Abbotsbury
Cerne
WINCHESTER

SHERBORNE

18 Dioceses and principal monasteries. The names of dioceses are marked in square boxes and the boundaries are marked by dotted lines. The monasteries are represented by the discs. The map indicates where most of the population lived

19 A church that shows the influence of Norman architects. It is at Iffley in Oxfordshire, and the dog-tooth carving around the door and windows is characteristic of Norman builders

The upsurge of interest in monasteries did not come until the middle of the tenth century. A similar revival of interest was taking place in France where the monastery at Cluny was the most famous of several that tried to re-establish the simple daily routine ordered by Benedict. The French ideas were known and adopted in this country, fitting in well with the desire to revitalise English monasteries. The first of this new era of monasteries was created by Dunstan, who was made Abbot of Glastonbury in Somerset in 940. The monks he trained were later promoted to monasteries and churches throughout Wessex, so that Dunstan greatly influenced the revival of all kinds of church life. Two of his more active students were Oswald, who founded, amongst others, the great monastery at Ramsey, and Ethelwold who became Bishop of Winchester. He used this high office to take over some of the former sites of monasteries within the lands conquered by the Danes and set up new monasteries. The largest of these new foundations were at Ely, Peterborough and Thorney. These were exceptional, however, in that the revival of the monasteries did not extend far beyond southern England—a century later, Crowland was the only monastery in Lincolnshire, Leicestershire, Nottinghamshire, Derbyshire and Yorkshire.

Numbers were not everything, though. The whole Church was affected in time as monks replaced the ordinary clergy as bishops and other high ranking officers of the Church. Every diocese between 975 and 1066 came under the control of a bishop who had also been a monk at some time, and they tried to train the parish priests to the same standards of self-discipline and enthusiasm as was found in the monasteries. In this way, the renewed life of the monasteries revitalised the Church, which carried it through the upheavals of the Norman conquest with few immediate changes.

20 Canterbury Cathedral. The emphasis is on height and light

Norman Conquest

The Normans were accustomed to bishops and priests playing a more active role in the country than they found in England. The bishops were the men of power in Normandy, not the abbots, and were seen to be powerful. The reason for this had little to do with religion and arose from the fact that only priests could read and write—the first Norman kings certainly could not. Many young men trained as priests who had only a faint interest in being priests but who wanted to be able to read. They then became the clerks and secretaries of the nobles with

21 The medieval wish to make a building that seemed light and lofty is seen once again in Tewkesbury Abbey in Gloucestershire

22 The long sink in the centre of this picture was where the monks at Gloucester washed before meals. Yet even here the ceiling has elaborate fan vaulting, instead of plain blocks of stone

large estates to run, and carried out their church duties in a careless way, if at all. The Normans had strict ideas of the importance of rank, and rewarded faithful servants. It suited both ideas to use bishoprics to reward their secretaries, regardless of their religious virtue. Just as the Norman barons who had come with the conquest were rewarded with large estates, so also were the bishops. In time they became very wealthy and powerful, and were among the king's chief advisers.

All this took some time to take effect, and was a snowballing process. Its effect on the Church took even longer to become obvious. As indicated already, the English Church was full of enthusiasm at the time of the conquest, and the monasteries continued to encourage the parish priests and people. The bishops set over them were Normans and often left the priests and abbots to carry on as they wanted. This was bound to cause trouble in time. The abbots had no one to turn to when difficulties arose, since the bishops were not interested, and gradually the idleness of the bishops spread to others in the Church. By the end of the twelfth century, all too many priests went through the motions of taking services,

23 Wood carving was extensively used to decorate churches. These pew ends are at Tenterden in Kent (*left*) and Crowcombe, Somerset (*right*)

baptising babies and burying the dead, without much thought of what they were doing or why. In this they were copying the bishops, who attended their cathedrals only on important occasions, leaving everything else to their deputies.

William Longchamp was just such a man. He began his career in the Church as a clerk. He became Chancellor in 1189 and justiciar in 1190, the most important posts in governing England. He therefore became regent when Richard I went off on the crusade, and ruled England. As a reward, he was made Bishop of Ely in 1190, and also, at Richard's request to the Pope, papal legate, which meant he ruled the Church in England. He was not a very lovable character, being over-confident, over-fond of power, tactless and anxious to use his power for the benefit of his family. He openly despised English people. A contemporary wrote, 'The laity found him more than a king, the clergy more than a pope, and both an intolerable tyrant'. This bishop made frequent journeys round the country with

33

his own troops, quartering them at monasteries. He strengthened his castles, which included the Tower of London, hired foreign troops, and collected heavy taxes to pay for it all. His career is an example of how the Church lost control over its own leaders, with disastrous consequences at a later date.

It should not be thought that all the bishops were evil men to behave in such a way. The trouble was that the king of England was able to take over the bishopric system and use it for his own purposes. The kings had nothing against the Church either, though they had their own way of showing respect for it. They needed the services of an educated civil service to be able to govern their lands in England and France, the priests were the only large body of literate people organised throughout these lands and were taken over so far as was necessary. Increasingly, the kings took over appointing bishops, and only appointed those they could rely on. The Church was deprived of its leaders without having any replacements. It was still ruled by these leaders, but they were seldom capable of leading effectively. Where there was a choice between what the Church ought to do and what the king wanted, the bishops normally did the latter. One who refused to carry out the king's orders was Thomas à Becket, Archbishop of Canterbury, who was murdered in his cathedral in 1174 at the king's suggestion. It is notable that he was later made a saint, as if few bishops dared to defy kings. By this time, a renewed revival was sweeping through the monasteries, which will be referred to shortly.

24   The murder of Thomas à Becket in 1170 by the four knights. The Archbishop's resistance to the king was an attempt to win back for the Church control over its own affairs

Despite the difficulties created by control at the top being taken over by the kings, the eleventh and twelfth centuries were a period of church building on a scale that had not been seen before. This was so both in the quantity of buildings and in their design. Very many Saxon churches were rebuilt, especially in the growing towns, such as York, Bristol, Norwich and Coventry. A visit to such cathedrals as Gloucester and Durham will illustrate better than words the graceful effects that builders were beginning to master.

Cistercian Monasteries

The French monastery at Cluny had become rich by 1100, and so had most of the other reformed monasteries. The monks lived too well, and elaborate ceremony in the services had taken the place of personal devotion. The monasteries ceased to influence the people outside, and were treated with indifference or contempt. The revolt against this again came from a French monastery, this time at Citeaux. It started in 1098 but its fame began when an Englishman, Stephen Harding, became its abbot in 1109. He drew up the rules that were the basis of the Cistercian order of monks, which transformed the popular idea of a monk in very few years. Some idea of their rules might make this hard to realise.

The monks believed in making life as hard for themselves as they could. In choosing the site for a new monastery, they were only to accept wild and undeveloped land in lonely places, and they had to develop it themselves. The Benedictine monks employed servants to do the dirty work, Cistercians were to do their own. Only one meal a day was allowed, which was a pound of bread, a choice of vegetables and fish or eggs. A drink of water was allowed in the evening. These rations were increased in the summer, when more outdoor work was done, to include a supper of bread and salad or raw fruit. A monk's clothing was a coarse, woollen habit, undyed (which gave Cistercians the nickname of 'white monks'). The simplicity extended to church, where crosses were wooden, candlesticks iron and no ornaments or statues were allowed. The purpose of it all was to allow as much time as they could for prayer and reading, yet supplying all their needs themselves.

Bernard (of Clairvaux) joined the new order in 1112 and became an enthusiastic member of it. Three hundred Cistercian monasteries were founded in the following forty years, twenty-five of them in England. The first to be set up in England was Waverley Abbey in Surrey, founded in 1128. The rapid growth of Cistercian abbeys, however, grew out of Rievaulx Abbey in Yorkshire, founded in 1131 by Bernard's secretary William, himself an Englishman. The monastery was built 'in a place of horror and vast solitude', and life was harsh, especially for new-comers. A description of it, as if by a novice, reads:

Our food is scanty, our garments rough; our drink is from the stream and our sleep often upon our book. Under our tired limbs there is but a mat; when sleep is sweetest we must rise at a bell's bidding. . . Self-will has no scope; there is no moment for idleness or dissipation ... Everywhere peace, everywhere serenity, and a marvellous freedom from the tumult of the world. Such unity and concord is there among the brethren that each thing seems to belong to all and all to each.

The Cistercians attracted many new members. Numbers at Rievaulx increased from twenty-five in 1131 to over three hundred by 1143, and this was not unusual. Later on, many well-wishers made generous gifts of land, which the monks developed. They were particularly skilful at running iron works and in producing wool. The money was used to replace temporary huts with graceful stone buildings, and to help those in need. A great plague swept England and France in 1194 and refugees looked to the monasteries for help. Many ill and starving people in Yorkshire went to Fountains Abbey, where the monks built temporary huts from branches, fed the starving and nursed the ill in their hospital. Monasteries had always tried to help people outside, and the Cistercians carried on the tradition.

Much of the rest of the Church, however, was less active either in worship of God or service of men. The bishops were too wealthy, the priests too poor and all too idle to be leaders of people. The main exceptions to this generalisation were the

25 Tintern Abbey on the river Wye, as it now appears. The church was built in the shape of the cross, and the open square in the angle of the church was the cloister, where the monks could walk and think

26 An artist's impression of how Tintern looked in the fifteenth century. It is viewed from a point at ninety degrees to fig. 25, and the cloister is in the centre of the picture

friars following the example of Francis of Assisi, who lived in Italy in the early thirteenth century. He gave up all wealth and possessions, begged for his food and had no home. Being this free of responsibilities, he was able to travel about, preaching, teaching and nursing the sick, especially the dreaded lepers. He was soon followed by others, and the Franciscan Order was formed in 1223. Organisation was simple, and many friars settled in the poor districts of the growing industrial towns. They came to England in 1224, and had built houses in the

27 A fourteenth-century scene of needy people arriving at a monastery for help. The cripple is barefoot, and the leper carries a begging bowl and warning rattle. The gate-kepper is giving them a blessing, while keeping a wary eye on the leper

28 (*left*) Only the Cellarer could hold the keys to the wine cellar. Is he sampling the vintage or having an unauthorised drink?

29 (*below*) A medieval church at Lead in Yorkshire. There are no houses anywhere near now, and the abandoned church is in the middle of a field

30 A friar preaching to a small crowd, a scene drawn in the fourteenth century. The congregation seem well dressed

sixteen largest towns by 1230. Another order of friars, the Dominicans, came to England in 1221 and also had houses in the main towns. These buildings were bases from which to set out on their journeys, and often became schools and hospitals as well. (Monks and friars were the only people to take an active interest in these matters. Their schools encouraged the development of the English language, and some of their buildings developed into universities, as at Oxford and Cambridge. In centuries when there were no doctors, as such, the friars and monks led the way in caring for the sick, and courageously tackled leprosy and mental illness.) The friars were welcomed. The Bishop of Lincoln wrote in 1239 that they 'illuminate our whole country with the bright light of their preaching and teaching'. Their emphasis on preaching led to many churches having extra aisles added to the nave to make room for the listeners. The friars showed their determination to help people by living in the worst parts of the towns, instead of a bishop's palace, and the poor were impressed by the friars' concern for them.

The friars represented the Church's concern for the underprivileged and suffering. However, the Church was less sympathetic to the members of the Jewish faith living in England. They had come at the time of the conquest and were given royal protection. They had a reputation for being successful in business, and lent their wealth to anyone needing a loan. The rates of interest were high, usually $43\frac{1}{3}\%$. Some of the Jews were exceedingly wealthy. Aaron of Lincoln lent money to people in twenty-five counties in the twelfth century, and his clients included Lincoln Cathedral, the Abbeys of Peterborough and St Albans, and nine Cistercian monasteries (which is an indication of the scale on which the Church employed architects and builders.) It took twenty years to sort out the accounts after his death in 1185.

The Jews' wealth, and their contempt for Christianity, made them unpopular. This unpopularity burst out in savage attacks on occasions. An incident during the coronation of Richard I in 1189 led to the burning and plunder of Jewish houses which went on all night, and many of the Jews were killed. The violence spread to other towns in the winter months, and similar horrors took place in Lynn, Norwich, Lincoln and Stamford, while in York, 150 people took refuge in the castle, but died. The survivors stayed in England but the communities were never to regain their former strength. Kings continued to extract as much money as they could, and life for the Jews became hedged around with restrictions and public dislike. Finally, they were expelled from England in 1290. No Christian could be proud of such bitterness and lack of restraint. Similar scenes took place on the crusades to recapture Palestine from the Moslems, where respect for the country as the Holy Land was forgotten in the passion to kill the enemy.

Wealth and Idleness

The Church as a whole became increasingly wealthy in the fourteenth and fifteenth centuries. Bishops had vast estates and could readily finance the building of their own palaces. The larger monasteries had also been given lands or other property and had large incomes. The responsibilities of managing these estates took up much of the time and enthusiasm of the leaders of the Church. At the other extreme, the parish priests were too poor to carry out their work properly in many cases. These men were seldom fully trained, and could offer little comfort or instruction to the people in their care.

Many complaints about behaviour of the clergy can be found. A bishop of Exeter accused the cathedral priests of 'laughing, giggling and other insolences during divine service itself'. At Ripon in Yorkshire, eight clerks were publicly stripped of all signs of being connected with the Church in 1302 for a mixture of murder, robbery and sacrilege. Six years later, the Archbishop of York noted 'Ripon Minster is becoming a den of thieves, a common market where lying and deceit are practised all the time', and ordered that the nave should no longer be used for business.

Increasingly people went to church only out of habit, for the enthusiasm of earlier times was dead. The leaders of the Church behaved as minor princes and were content with things as they were. Many parish priests were apparently indifferent to the needs of their people. Even the monasteries no longer followed the strict rules of their orders, but became wealthy and lazy, setting a bad example,

31 A group of invalids, including a woman leper, are shown the relic of a saint. People put a lot of faith in the healing powers of relics but this faith was abused at times

if any at all. There may have been some priests and monks whose love of God and those around them was of the old, high standard but they have left little evidence. The majority of churchmen were content to live life like everyone else, and their religious activities were meaningless to themselves and to other people. At times when the Church had been active, ordinary people and Church leaders alike had gone on pilgrimages to see relics of the saints or other venerated places (the chapel at Walsingham in Norfolk, for example) as ways of increasing their understanding of religion; now, though the pilgrimages continued, they were largely looked on as holidays. Some protested against the Church's complacent attitude to such changes but the Church was now wealthy and powerful enough to crush any opposition.

4 Reformation and Disagreement

The Lollards

There were many critics of the Church at the end of the fourteenth century. The most influential of them was John Wyclif, a leading lecturer at Oxford University. He had been present at the parliament of 1371, when two friars had argued that all priests and monks should be as poor as they. This was an idea that appealed to Wyclif and many others, for the Church owned a third of all the land in England and Wales. Increasingly, Wyclif felt this was leading far too many monks and priests into a life of luxury and idleness, which was in sharp contrast both to the way most people had to live and to the way Christ had lived.

32 Mount Grace Priory in Yorkshire was built by the Carthusians in the fifteenth century. Each monk had his own house and garden, and the whole community only saw each other in church. One of its first priors, Prior Love, wrote pamphlets against the Lollards

33 John Wyclif criticised the slackness of many priests and monks, and encouraged people to read the Bible and think for themselves

During the 1370s, Wyclif developed these thoughts in lectures and pamphlets. He had a number of supporters at Oxford until 1384, when Church leaders forced these lecturers to abandon Wyclif. He had growing support in other parts of the country, among poorer priests and many others outside the Church. Some of these travelled about preaching, and soon attracted the nickname of Lollards.

There was at Leicester a priest called William of Swynderby [in the days of Richard II (1377–99), who preached] against the clergy saying they were bad, and as the rest of the sect [Lollards] said, parishioners need not pay tithes to the impure, to non-residents, or those prevented from teaching and preaching by ignorance or inaudibility, for the other Wycliffites said tithes were a voluntary gift and payment to evil-livers was connivance. He also preached that men might ask for payment of debt but . . . excommunication for non-payment of tithes was extortion and that one who lived contrary to God's law was no priest though ordained.

Such and other teachings and heresies pleased the people and won their affection . . .

John Bukkyngham, Bishop of Lincoln, had wind of this and promptly suspended him from all preaching in chapel, church or graveyard, excommunicating any who should listen to him, and sending notices of this to various churches. William set himself up a pulpit between two millstones which stood for sale outside the chapel in the High Street . . . You would have seen crowds from all over the town and country flocking to hear him more than ever before the excommunication.

'Non-residents' were preists who seldom visited their parishes but demanded the tithes, even so. They put in their place clerks who could hardly read the prayer

43

book services and who often gabbled their way through the service as quickly as they could. A person excommunicated from the Church could not attend any services, which was regarded as a serious punishment. Wyclif maintained that, although a man might have been trained as a priest, he did not deserve to be treated as one if he behaved in an unchristian way.

This account was written at the end of the fourteenth century by a canon at St Mary's Abbey, Leicester, who was one of the people being attacked by the Lollards. He was not fond of them for that reason, and was pleased when William was found guilty of heresy (teaching things that were contrary to what the Church believed) and sentenced to be burnt. William was saved by the intervention of John of Gaunt, who agreed with many of Wyclif's views. The brutal penalty of burning at the stake did not put an end to the critics, rather their numbers slowly increased during the fifteenth century. The Church did little to reform itself and the old abuses continued. The Lollards, on the other hand, developed their ideas on how the Church should behave. Wyclif had set in hand the first translation of the Bible into English. It was finished in 1396 (after Wyclif's death) and many copies must have been made by hand as 170 still exist. Increasingly, in the fifteenth century, groups of people met to read and discuss the Bible, and came to the same conclusions that Wyclif had reached years before. Such groups met in many parts of England in the 1490s, and in Ayrshire. These people wanted to hear more preaching about what the Bible should mean to them, were puzzled about the meaning of the communion service, and wanted their priests to believe in what they were doing. The reaction of Church leaders to such thinking was to try to ban Wyclif's Bible and discourage people by harsh treatment. As before, such methods only increased the number of people who wanted reforms.

The critics were not alone. Martin Luther started a campaign to reform the Church in Germany, for which he was excommunicated in 1521. Soon after, many of the German churches broke away from the Roman Catholic church and formed the Lutheran church. This began the break-up of the Church in western Europe, where, until this time, everyone had gone to identical services in a church for whom the Bishop of Rome (the pope) had ultimate responsibility. The Lutheran church was known as a protestant church, since it started because Luther protested at some of the practices of the Roman church, even though he had no quarrel with the basic teachings. He was soon followed by John Calvin in Switzerland, whose ideas on belief and ceremonies were far more radical and led to the formation of another protestant church.

34 (*opposite*) The title-page of the translation 'out of Douche and Latyn in to Englishe' by Miles Coverdale. It was printed in 1535 and met with considerable opposition. These difficulties account for the first quotation—'Praie for us, that the worde of God maie have fre passage'

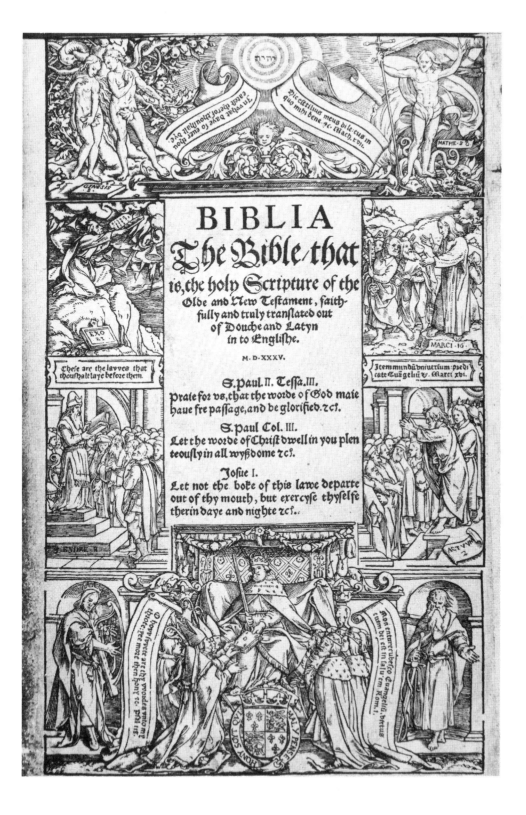

The English Reformation

England and Wales also broke away from the Roman Catholic church but the break took many years during and after the reign of Henry VIII, and the reasons for the change were very complex. As has been seen, there were already many people in the country who wanted reform, and the news of events in Germany and Switzerland reinforced the reformers. Few of them, however, thought that so drastic a step as throwing off the control of the pope was necessary. Henry VIII, although he was responsible for the break with Rome, was a loyal Catholic and wrote a book against Luther's ideas, for which he was rewarded by the pope with the title Defender of the Faith (which still appears on coins in abbreviated Latin as FD). The reformation in England was started by Henry but it was not done for any religious reason.

Henry's first wife, Catherine, had failed to bear a son as heir to the throne, which mattered more to Henry than anything else. He wished to divorce her and marry Anne Boleyn. This divorce could only be allowed by the pope, and he refused, being under pressure from Henry's European rivals who included Catherine's nephew. Without a divorce, no child born to Anne could legally be heir to the throne. Henry hoped that his Chancellor, Cardinal Wolsey, would be able to arrange a divorce for him but Wolsey failed and would have been put on trial for his failure had he not died first. When he failed, Henry began to put pressure on the pope through parliament. A series of acts were passed from 1529 onwards, and each one took away a larger part of the pope's authority in England, but the pope was not to be intimidated. At last, in 1534, the Act of Supremacy made Henry head of the Church in England in place of the pope, and all Church leaders had to swear their loyalty to him. This offended many Catholics, and a few, of whom the most respected was Sir Thomas More, refused to regard a layman as head of the Church, even if he was a king. They were executed.

So Henry had brought about the division between the English and the Roman churches, not for religious reasons but out of political and personal necessity. In doing so, he had carried out a number of reforms the Lollards had wanted, such as making non-residence illegal. He still insisted, however, that the Catholic church was the only church in England, and the Six Articles passed by parliament in 1539 laid down the essentials of its teaching and the death penalty for any who disagreed. The reformation up to this point was an unsatisfactory affair. The Church in England was no longer truly Catholic since the pope's authority was no longer recognised, yet it was not Protestant—no other deviation from Roman Catholic teaching was permitted. The changes that had been made angered loyal Catholics who could not accept anyone but the pope as head of the Church, and angered the reformers who wanted far more sweeping alterations. The pendulum of change and counter-change swung several times before Elizabeth I ordered it to a standstill, as will be seen.

The political reformation was taken further when the monasteries were closed at the king's command in 1536 and 1539. Reasons were trumped up for every monastery, usually along the lines that the monks (or nuns) were lazy or corrupt, and in some cases this was true. The main reason was that Henry needed money urgently and, being head of the Church, he could take the lands and buildings after he had shut down the monasteries. This undermined the foundations of the Church as they had existed in England for a thousand years, and was bound to cause considerable upheaval. The immediate consequences were unpleasant. Many monks and nuns were suddenly without home or money and had to hunt around for some work. Care for the ill and the starving was no longer provided, and many thousands of people who had worked for the monasteries were made redundant. Even the roads became worse, for monasteries had frequently made themselves responsible for roads and bridges near them. No one took over the social work of the monasteries, and people were worse off because of that. On the other hand, the land and buildings were made available for other purposes. Many monks and nuns became teachers, since they were educated, and there was an increase in the numbers of children (mostly boys) who had the chance of some education. Monastery buildings also became schools. Bristol Grammar School began in 1532 in the monastic hospital of St Bartholomew, and retained the buildings after the dissolution. Industry also benefitted from the release of labour and buildings. A large brass works was developed in the ruins of Tintern Abbey, Monmouthshire, while in Wiltshire John Stumpe installed more than a hundred hand looms in Malmesbury Abbey. Increased employment and educational opportunities were of great benefit to the country in time, but were little comfort to the monks turned out by dissolution. The people who had formerly looked to the monasteries when times were bad, now had nowhere to turn.

Demands for More Reforms

There was one other far-reaching consequence of the dissolution of the monasteries. In times past, the people who became monks were normally of the thoughtful kind, not put off at the thought of spending a lifetime reading and thinking about God and how he should best be served. Services in the parish churches, by contrast, followed the same pattern each week and were meant to enable people to worship God in a brief time away from the long hours of work. Those who thought deeply about religion did not find enough in the prayer book services to satisfy them (both the friars and the Lollards had been popular for their emphasis on preaching before the monasteries were closed) and were bound to expect changes in the way services were planned.

Some slight changes came while Henry was still king. A new translation of the Bible in more modern English was completed in 1537 by William Tyndale and Miles Coverdale and the prayer book in English was used from 1545. People could now understand for themselves what was being said, instead of having it in Latin. Edward VI's advisers went further by ordering the destruction of all statues and other decorations in churches, and by preparing a prayer book (in 1552) which was not only Protestant but bitterly anti-Catholic. The pace of change

35 Ridley, Latimer and many more were burnt at the stake for their protestant views in 1555–56. Their deaths caused many people to sympathise with their beliefs

was too great for many, and there was a battle between government troops and loyal Catholics at Clyst St Mary, near Exeter. The west countrymen were trying to stop changes being forced on them, but were no match for trained troops. Queen Mary tried to restore order by a return to the Catholic church. The mass was restored in 1553, and England was accepted back into the Roman Catholic church in the following year. There were many, however, who had welcomed the service in English and the chance to think for themselves. They were convinced the Roman Catholic church was wrong in some of its teachings and Mary was forced to revive the policy of burning heretics to quell the opposition. Mostly bishops were burnt in 1555–6, and also about 270 men and women who were not priests. Far from stamping out the Protestants, many waverers were greatly impressed at the courage and convictions of those who faced burning for their beliefs. The attempt to turn the clock back had failed.

Creation of the Church of England
Elizabeth I became queen in 1558 and was determined to settle matters so that people should know what it was safe to believe. She made herself head of the Church in England instead of the pope. A new prayer book was issued which was

Protestant without being anti-Catholic. Some parts were left deliberately ambiguous so that Catholics and Protestants could interpret it in whatever way pleased them. Elizabeth had in this way formed the Protestant Church of England that is still the largest church in the country. Everyone had to attend church and could be fined for non-attendance, but most people accepted the settlement. Some Catholic priests travelled from one Catholic house to another, saying mass, but they went in fear of their lives. There were also some extreme Protestants who could not accept a prayer book of any kind, who met secretly. Most of the country, however, settled down to the new Protestant church which had been created out of thirty years of argument and bloodshed. Scotland began its own reformation in 1559, and the presbyterian Church of Scotland became the new church in 1560. Only Ireland remained loyal to the Roman Catholic church, which had replaced the Celtic customs centuries before.

Dissenters

Elizabeth was not entirely successful in keeping the Church of England united. Some Roman Catholic families refused to have anything to do with it and suffered accordingly. There was also a number of people who had expected Elizabeth to reform still more and were disappointed when she did not. These reformers became known as dissenters, a word that meant they did not agree with the Church of

36 Archbishop Cranmer lived through and assisted the changes made by Henry VIII and Edward VI, and was finally burned for his protestant beliefs in 1556

37 Elizabeth I (1558–1603), first head of the Church of England. She attempted a middle course between reformers and those wishing to keep all the old ways, and succeeded in calming religious passions for a while

England. There were many groups of dissenters and, as they had to meet in secret, few details are known of them. Some were drawn to the presbyterian kind of service and church control, with elders in place of bishops. The largest group were guided by the writings of Robert Browne, and were known as Brownists, Separatists or Independents. They felt that each congregation should run its own affairs according to what they understood from the Bible and what they felt God meant them to do. There was no room for bishops in such a view, nor for prayer books. Frequent bouts of persecution led to many of them being imprisoned in the 1580s, and some were hung. Many sailed to Holland at the end of the sixteenth century to escape persecution, and it was from there that some set out in 1620 to set up a new country in America, where all religious ideas would be tolerated.

There was certainly no room for Catholics or dissenters in an England governed by James I, who forced those who would not attend their parish church to leave the country. His only contribution was to authorise a new translation of the Bible, which was completed in 1611 and was the only one in general use for over three centuries. Secretly, however, the Independents continued to meet. Groups of other sects also met by stealth, chief among them being the Baptists. Many of these joined the rebel armies when the king and parliament failed to agree and civil war broke out. After the war, Oliver Cromwell (an Independent) tried to make it possible for all non-Catholic sects to continue with their customs side by side. Bishops were abolished and Westminster Abbey became an Independent church, but many clergymen of the Church of England were allowed to use the prayer book undisturbed.

The attempt at toleration did not outlast Cromwell's death in 1658. It was too new an idea. At this time in Europe it was taken for granted that there could only be one kind of religion in a country. Toleration between several groups was an idea that the Independents could accept, for they struggled only for the right to behave as they thought the Bible commanded them, but few others could understand such a notion. Accordingly, when Charles II came to the throne in 1660, the Church of England was immediately re-established and a renewed attack on all other groups soon followed. About 2,000 dissenting preachers were removed from their churches in 1662, and, later, their congregations were prohibited from meeting and their schools were closed. Individual dissenters were constantly being arrested and imprisoned, and an example of this was the frequent goalings of the Independent John Bunyan, author of *Pilgrim's Progress*. To take another example, over 10,000 members of the newly formed Society of Friends (or Quakers) were arrested between 1661–89. Such persecution continued into the eighteenth century and, except for treatment of the Catholics and Jews, was the last major persecution of religious groups in England. There was no similar campaign in Scotland which was a separate country until united with England and Wales in 1707, by which time the worst of the persecution was over. Ireland was also separate and remained Catholic, though there was a growing community of Protestants in the north. These were descended from settlers who went to take advantage of farm land confiscated from the Irish in 1607. Many of the settlers were Presbyterians from Scotland and dedicated Protestants from London, seeking a land where they could carry on with their beliefs unhindered.

Summary

A revolution had come about in Church affairs in the 200 years after 1500. At its simplest, the Roman Catholic church that had been the only church in England and Wales had been replaced by the protestant Church of England, set up by king and protected by parliament. Roman Catholics were now the hunted and hated few, liable to many penalties for their beliefs. The Church of England had been designed to appeal to a very wide range of Protestant views, but had not appealed to all. Its compromise between the customary Catholic ritual in church services and the Protestant preference for extreme simplicity had appealed no more to dissenters than it had to devout Catholics. There were in 1700 a large number of dissenting groups, for whom the prayer book services of the Church of England were too binding. Some of the dissenters in time formed separate churches, such as the Baptists and Quakers. Other groups, for example the Familists, did not last beyond the seventeenth century. England and Wales had moved from a time when there was just one church, to having one church established by law and a great many outside the law's protection. Slowly people had to learn to tolerate each other's religious views.

One group who were not tolerated in the seventeenth century were the witches. Many people, both educated and ignorant, firmly believed that witch-craft was an evil that should be stamped out. Many old women were rounded up and executed for casting spells. The witch-hunts were most active in James I's reign and when parliament ruled England—over 200 witches were executed in the eastern counties from 1645 to 1647. The last execution occurred in Exeter in 1685 and the crime of witchcraft was abolished in 1736. It is very hard to say whether witch-craft had much support as a religion.

Social Concern

Up until the time that the monasteries were dissolved, monks and nuns had carried out much charitable work in caring for the sick and providing education. When the monasteries were closed, they were absorbed into society, where many carried on the work. By about 1700, people who thought deeply about religion and would once have joined a monastery now met in each other's homes for study and discussion, and their understanding of Christianity was reflected in how they behaved. The Celtic tradition in the English Church was still strong.

The dissenters ran their own schools from the end of the seventeenth century, and the quality of education far surpassed anything available in other schools.

38 This lead tablet holds a curse against Sarah Ellis, and is a sign of seventeenth–century witchcraft. Any old woman might be suspected of having evil powers and little evidence was needed to have her condemned to death

New subjects were introduced, such as modern languages and geography, that were still unknown in some grammar schools a century later.

The Quakers in particular became the champions of social justice. George Fox, their founder, wrote many letters encouraging employers to pay fair wages to their servants, denouncing the Cornish wreckers, wanting inns closed to reduce drunkenness, opposing the death penalty for cattle thieves and complaining about conditions in prisons. Another Quaker suggested in 1660 that every parish should have its own 'poor man's office' (what we would call a labour exchange) where jobs could be advertised. John Bellers went still further, wanting free medicines and hospital treatment, and each parish to pay its own doctors. The social work of the Quakers continued and extended the work formerly done by the friars and monasteries. It was as if the best aspects of the monastic life had been released from the monasteries by the reformation and could now be done by anyone. The alternating waves of enthusiasm and neglect that had marked the monasteries soon began to wash over the reformed churches also.

5 Politics and Methodists

The eighteenth century began with a lack of interest in religion, or so it appeared after the turmoil of the previous two centuries. The strong feelings and bloodshed aroused then left many people exhausted, and not very impressed with the Church. It had shown a strange way of loving one's enemy, and it was even stranger to regard as an enemy someone sharing the same religion.

The State of the Church

The Church of England was the dominant denomination in 1700, and the great majority of people attended services where the Book of Common Prayer was used. The services were in English and followed a regular pattern each week. Although attended by the whole village community, the squire and the vicar were the leading landowners of the village and many people felt that the church was there to support them, and not to provide for the needs of the people. Even so, everyone went to church and this affected the way they lived. The basic morals of society were known and accepted. Every village had its lawbreakers but normally life in the village reflected the Church's teaching. Conditions in the towns were different for, instead of everyone working in the same industry (agriculture), there were many industries and no common bond between people. Life in the towns was less healthy and less pleasant in every way. This was a problem that only became serious after the middle of the century, when the population began to increase rapidly and revolutions in farming and industry led to more people living in towns.

The other denominations suffered under many legal obstacles. The dissenters had been allowed by the Toleration Act in 1689 to build their own chapels and to hold the services they thought right. They could not take part in local government, however, or hold commissions in the army—they were not trusted. Their children could not be educated in the grammar schools nor go on to the only English universities of Oxford and Cambridge, and even their own academies were banned from 1714–19. Many dissenters, especially Quakers, turned their attention to trade and industry, since so many other professions were closed to them. Their honesty and hard work soon made them successful, and this, to the money-conscious minds of the time, made them respectable. The laws against the dissenters were increasingly ignored as the century wore on, and they were more widely accepted by society.

It was very different for the Roman Catholics. The laws against them were daunting, and it was all too easy for a rabble-rouser to whip up hatred of the

39 A sermon being preached in an Anglican church in the eighteenth century. Most of the congregation seem well dressed and literate

Catholics after the unhappy three-year reign of the Catholic James II (1685–8). Even as late as 1780, Lord Gordon was able to collect a crowd in the streets of London to protest against relaxing the laws against Catholics. (The crowd rioted and held London in a ferment for a week, by which time 458 people had been killed or wounded.) The full list of penalties against Catholics would take up too much space but some examples are that a priest could be fined £200 for being in the country at all and could be charged with treason for saying mass; Catholics could be fined £20 a month for not attending the Church of England; could be neither lawyer nor doctor; could not sit in parliament or take part in local government and could not travel more than 5 miles (8 km) from home without a licence. The penalties were seldom imposed in full but were there. Most Catholics were working people living in towns, a section of the population that was either ignored or despised in this century.

Treatment of the Jews was a little better, largely because there were few of them in the country. They were allowed to worship in their own way, but could not own land or be naturalised as British subjects.

The laws against all these groups were seldom enforced and yet were not removed from the statute book. The governments could well remember past troubles and were afraid to abandon these protective laws. Ordinary people were far more tolerant and, except for isolated outbursts like the Gordon riots, were prepared to accept the fact that people could worship in many different ways.

The Church of England

Early in the eighteenth century the laws were still recent and the minority denominations were somewhat subdued. The Church of England covered the country and, being so large, was full of variations. It could still not prevent itself being used in politics. Bishops had been the civil servants of kings in the middle ages; now they were the supporters in the House of Lords/of the politicians who had had them made bishops. Men were appointed from 1714 onwards who would support the new king George from Hanover and the Whig Party that he favoured in parliament. 'Support' meant being in London for the six months in the year that parliament sat, and putting pressure on the parsons in the diocese at elections to see that they helped the Whig candidates. The bishops of the middle years of the century were all men who had written in support of the Whigs or the king, or who had served the king and his ministers by being ambassadors abroad. A popular song, now often found in books of nursery rhymes, highlighted the political motives of many vicars. It was called the *The Vicar of Bray* and part of it went:

> I turned a cat-in-pan once more,
> And so became a Whig, Sir.
> And this preferment I procured
> From our new faith's defender.

There was still much jockeying for further promotion once a man became a bishop, for some of the bishoprics were worth ten times as much in cash as others.

The church could not be well served with such men at the top. They had little time to devote to the work of their dioceses and some treated that side of their work with contempt. Bishop Hoadly visited his diocese once in the six years he was Bishop of Bangor, and never went near Hereford in the two years he was the bishop there. On the other hand, many bishops did the best they possibly could in the time that was left to them after carrying out their political duties. The fault lay in the fact that politicians could choose the bishops.

The political influences reached beyond the bishops. Most parish churches had vicars appointed by the local landowner, who naturally chose someone who agreed with his views. The younger sons of noble families were frequently appointed to the parish church which, as one of them remarked, was 'a pretty easy way of dawdling away one's time'. Such vicars were often scholarly but lacked religious enthusiasm. Indeed, enthusiasm was frowned on as being quite unsuitable in church. Religion was a comfortable matter, not something that ought to raise awkward problems, such as taking notice of the appalling poverty in some areas. Cosy religion was what appealed to the squires, and the Church of England obliged for most of the century.

Many of the parsons were as badly paid as ever. Early in the century the Archbishop of Canterbury had an annual income of £7,000; nearly 6,000 of the 10,000 parishes paid less than £50; 1,200 of them less than £20. Such payments did not attract the best candidates nor enable them to carry out their functions well. Bishop Burnet wrote early in the century:

The much greater part of those who come to be ordained are ignorant to a degree not to be apprehended by those who are not obliged to know it. The easiest part of knowledge is that to which they are the greatest strangers; I mean the plainest part of the Scriptures, which they say, in excuse for their ignorance, that their tutors in the Universities never mention the reading of

40 An eighteenth-century cartoon of an Anglican service. The sermon is no doubt being read in excellent English but has long since lost the attention of the congregation

to them, so that they can give no account, or at least a very imperfect one, of the contents even of the Gospels ... Politics and party eat out among us not only study and learning, but ... also a true sense of religion, with a sincere zeal in advancing that for which the Son of God both lived and died, and to which those who are received into holy orders have vowed to dedicate their lives and labours.

Such men were not likely to be able to help their parishioners in any way whatever. There were, therefore, all kinds of vicars, from those who were more concerned with politics than with their parishioners to those who really tried to help them, both by their services and by looking after them when times were bad. As a general rule, few demands were made on the vicars and few were at their best.

The dissenting churches were also quiet at the start of the century, though for different reasons. They had had to fight for the right to worship as they liked. Now that they had the right, they enjoyed it for a while, wondering whether

41 A service in Bath Abbey in 1788. The children are dressed alike and may be from local charity schools. There is a lack of seating and the adults are kneeling against the walls

persecution might start again. No political pressures could be brought to bear on them for each church was independent and either chose its own minister or was led by one of its own members. Most of these churches remained somewhat inward-looking for most of the eighteenth century, settling down after the earlier struggles. One major change in the pattern of services was the growing use of hymns sung by the congregation. Isaac Watts was the most prolific among many hymnwriters.

Philanthropy

It should not be thought that all church people closed their eyes to the needs of those around them. Much was done by individuals and societies to improve conditions for those who needed help. Captain Coram, ex-naval officer, started the Foundling Hospital in London in 1745 to care for the many hundreds of babies abandoned in the streets. Children were brought up there, and put out as apprentices when they were old enough so that they were equipped with the means to earn their own living. General Oglethorpe agitated about the scandalous conditions in debtors' prisons, as a result of which a society was formed in 1772 to pay off the debts and set the released men up in the American colony of Georgia. The last part did not survive long but 12,000 were released in the first thirty years. Others founded hospitals, dispensaries and lying-in hospitals (maternity homes); 154 were founded between 1700 and 1825.

Much was done in education too. The Society for Promoting Christian Knowledge was formed in 1698 to encourage the distribution of Bibles, and was responsible for starting many charity schools, as they were called. In Exeter, for example, the bishop set the ball rolling:

[In 1708] observing with concern the great number of the poor illiterate children, whose parents were not of ability to educate them, preached a sermon concerning the rules and measures of Alms-giving, and the manifold Advantages of Charity Schools for the Instruction and education of the poor of this city and other places of this Diocese; and out of zeal for his design his Lordship annexed to his excellent sermon a pious letter to his clergy, thereby exciting them to a greater zeal for this work of Piety and Charity: and the very next day after the sermon, a great number of the inhabitants of this city voluntarily subscribed for the erecting of Charity Schools within this place . . .

There were four schools by 1724, two for boys and two for girls. New clothing was provided once a year for each child, and the 'boys are taught to read and write and cast accounts: the girls to sew and knit: They all have Bibles, Common Prayer Books and Spelling Books given them and are examined every Sunday in their Catechism.'

Similar schools were being founded in every town at this time and, with all their limitations, did provide a few years of education for children who otherwise

59

42 Another eighteenth-century cartoon. The vicar is well fed and can afford to keep a horse, which he uses to collect the (by now) hated tithes. In contrast the farm worker has to carry the basket of vegetables on his back

would have had none at all. The same may be said of the Sunday schools which sprang up everywhere following the success of Robert Raikes' school in Gloucester in 1780. These provided a little learning for children who worked all day, the Bible being the textbook as it was the only book readily available. Other men were moved to attack such evils as slavery and the slave trade. Religion for much of the century is seen better through its achievements than through the activities of its leaders.

All denominations of the Church were out of touch with the poor in east London. As more towns grew, the same could be said of large areas of the Black Country and the north of England, and of more localised industrial regions such as the coal mines of Kingswood in Gloucestershire and the Cornish mines and fishing towns. The Church of England was divided into parishes and could not adapt itself to sudden influxes of people into a parish. Much more to the point, few vicars (or dissenting ministers) could understand the living and working conditions in industrial areas, and had little to say that was relevant. Mining areas were often avoided by the Church, and miners were all too well known for their drunkeness and brutality.

The Methodists

The people who faced up to this situation were methodists. These were drawn from the more serious members of both the Anglican and dissenting churches, and earned their nickname from the way in which they divided their time between prayer, Bible study, work and helping other people. They felt that life was too short and precious to waste any of it in idleness or luxury. Two such men converted Wales from a country largely indifferent to religion into the chapel-going, hymn-singing, Bible-quoting land that it still largely is. The two men were Howel Harris and Daniel Rowlands, and they travelled all over the country preaching with great enthusiasm and in language people could understand. Religion again meant something and could be adapted to daily life.

In England, similar direct preaching was attempted by a handful of vicars in their own churches, such as Henry Venn in Huddersfield, whom hundreds packed the church to hear, no matter what day of the week he preached. Such men were

43 William Wilberforce had this model of a slave ship made to show parliament the crowded conditions on the long passage across the Atlantic. The campaign was won eventually

few and completely missing from the new mining areas. A few methodists therefore decided to travel to other men's parishes and preach there. George Whitefield was one of the first of these who, where he found the parish church closed to him, preached in the open air. On such an occasion he addressed the colliers of Kingswood. He invited John Wesley to one of these gatherings in 1739, and convinced Wesley that he should preach to all people, regardless of parish boundaries.

So began John Wesley's tireless journeys around Britain preaching to whoever would listen. He was sometimes joined by his brother Charles, the hymnwriter, and sometimes by other methodists. These men needed considerable courage. The mining and other industrial areas were not so peaceful as rural villages. Work was hard and often dangerous, and living conditions were poor. There was much drunkeness and fighting. The following extract from John Wesley's diary illustrates the dangers he faced, and also his confidence in the value of what he was doing:

Thursday 4 [July, 1745]—I rode to Falmouth. About three in the afternoon I went to see a gentlewoman who had been long indisposed. Almost as soon as I was set down, the house was beset on all sides by an innumerable multitude of people. A louder or more confused noise could hardly be at the taking of a city by storm... The rabble roared, with all their throats, 'Bring out the Canorum! Where is the Canorum!' (an unmeaning word which the Cornish generally use instead of Methodist). No answer being given, they quickly forced open the outer door and filled the passage. Only a wainscot partition was between us, which was not likely to stand long ... When they began their work, with abundance of bitter imprecations, poor Kitty was utterly astonished, and cried out, 'O, Sir, what must we do?' I said, 'We must pray.' ... She asked, 'But, Sir, is it not better for you to hide yourself? to get into the closet?' I answered, 'No. It is best for me to stand just where I am'. Among those without were the crews of some privateers, which were lately come into the harbour. Some of these, being angry at the slowness of the rest, thrust them away, and coming up all together, set their shoulders to the inner door, and cried out, 'Avast, lads, avast!'. Away went all the hinges at once, and the door fell back into the room. I stepped forward at once into the midst of them, and said, 'Here I am. Which of you has anything to say to me? To which of you have I done any wrong? To you? or you? or you?' I continued speaking until I came ... into the middle of the street ...

He persuaded the crowd to listen to him, until it was time to leave Falmouth.

The gentlemen proposed sending for my horse to the door ... But on second thoughts they judged it not advisable to let me go out among the people again; so they chose to send my horse before me to Penryn, and to send me thither by water, the sea running close by the back of the house in which we were.

44 John Wesley speaking to a small crowd. The parish church is closed to him, so he has to stand on a tombstone while his audience are spread among the graves

It was not often as bad as that. Wesley and his followers were quickly able to convince most people of their genuine concern. The attacks and stone-throwing that greeted him in most parts of Britain in the 1740s were a thing of the past by 1750. Wesley told the crowds that God cared for them, and this gave people a new way of looking at life. The Celtic races of Wales and the north and south-west of England showed it first in joyful hymn-singing and enthusiastic attendance at the new chapels, which might be 10 miles (16 km) walk away from home. Many of the new methodists became preachers, despite the fact that they had not been to university and still worked at their old jobs. They were 'lay' preachers, that is, they were not ordained like the vicars and ministers of the other denominations. This was to lead to the formation of the Methodist church at the end of the century, a breakaway from the Anglican church that Wesley had hoped to avoid.

The Methodists attracted many members and had a profound influence on countless families. Belief in God gave men a purpose in life where before life had seemed pointless. They began to learn to read and write, often using the Bible and Wesley's hymns as text books. They gave up drinking to excess and took a pride in themselves. Attention was paid to the state of their homes and they sought better jobs. Whole industrial areas became more peacable and contented, an important change at a time when revolution was sweeping America, France and other countries. Experience of speaking in public as lay preachers led many men

63

45 This painting of a Methodist gathering was made in 1777. It was meant to poke fun at the kind of people that went to the open-air meetings, and at the unseemly surroundings for a service

to become leaders in trade unions early in the nineteenth century. Wesley's teaching, combined with his organising ability in seeing that there was adequate leadership for the converts, completely altered the way people lived, and was one of several reasons why the violence and restlessness of town life in the eighteenth century gave way to calmer and safer times in the nineteenth.

Wesley had become popular with large sections of the community by the time he grew old, as was seen when he revisited Falmouth in 1789. 'High and low now lined the street from one end of the town to the other, out of stark love and kindness, gaping and staring as if the king were going by.' He had also been accepted into some Church of England pulpits, Henry Venn's for example; the majority stayed closed to him even though he had been ordained as a priest in the Anglican church. They remained closed to Methodists, for the Church of England did not care for the enthusiasm of the new preachers, nor their working background. The Methodists were thus forced out of that church. The tide of change and a responsible attitude by church leaders was soon going to rise within the Church of England, and in the dissenting churches, leading to a time when the Church had some influence on everybody.

6 Churchmen and Church-going

The French Revolution in 1797 had overthrown both the French monarchy and, in Paris at least, the influence of the Catholic church. Napoleon had emerged as the new leader and by the beginning of the nineteenth century his armies were at war with Britain. The war dragged on until 1815, during which time many changes took place in Britain. The Methodist church continued to attract new members and its fervour was unwavering. The open-air meetings of large crowds had given way to crowded chapels. The influence of the Methodists was considerable. They were noted for their honesty and hard work, and many employers now

46 A service in a village church early in the nineteenth century. More seating has been provided and the congregation seems to be concentrating on what is being said

47 Few churches had organs. Instead the choir was accompanied by an orchestra. Thomas Hardy describes the trouble caused at one church when the changeover to an organ was made, in *Under the Greenwood Tree*

preferred to employ them, where fifty years before men had been fired for becoming Methodists. The fact that large numbers of people were committed to that church was one of several reasons for there being no revolution in England at this time, though living conditions were similar to conditions in France. The Methodist church, like the other dissenting churches, was largely organised by laymen, which gave many men training in administration, public speaking and self-government. This was to have considerable influence on the formation of trade unions, and dissenters were also active radicals in other matters.

Evangelical Movement

Changes had also come about in the established Church of England during the war years, and the changes influenced much of that church's activities for the rest of the century. The result of the changes was to make both clergymen and lay people more evangelical. They now stressed that it was important for each person to have a personal faith, mere membership of a church and regular attendance at its services were not enough. Vicars began again to be enthusiastic preachers and to look for a positive response from their congregations. This revival of enthusiasm for spreading a lively faith began at the end of the eighteenth century, though it had no leaders corresponding to the Wesleys among the Methodists. It was undoubtedly influenced by their activities, perhaps as an unconscious feeling that the Anglican church should be doing much the same. A group of men in Clapham, such as Henry Thornton, Granville Sharp and John Venn, were influential in encouraging this evangelical approach, especially during the war years. This was a revival within the church, and the bishops were able to guide the movement. It gradually spread throughout the church, and in so doing influenced the upper and middle classes who were the main attenders at parish churches. Since these were the leaders in government, industry and society, the evangelicals exerted a considerable influence over the country.

The evangelicals were, of course, regular attenders at church. They were strict about how they behaved, honest, trustworthy and hard-working. Life in this world, they thought, was but a training ground for eternity, and they would have to give account then of how they had behaved and what they had done with their time and money. Their hard work brought many of them wealth, and much of this was used to assist other people. A vast number of societies were formed in the nineteenth century, such as the Royal National Lifeboat Institution, formed in 1824, or the British and Foreign Bible Society, started in 1804 to make the Bible readily available in every language, Welsh being the first. All these humanitarian societies, whether obviously 'religious' or not, were generously supported by evangelical people, who felt it their duty to use their wealth to help others in need. They often thought that people were poor because they were thoughtless or extravagant, but they still helped.

It was their duty also to take a serious interest in public affairs, to read the Bible and to make Sunday a day of rest. Many families started the day with family prayers, and all of Sunday was set aside for going to church and reading serious books. All this meant that many people grew up having thought about the serious

48 Family prayers, and the servants have been summoned to join the family for the Bible reading. They do not all seem to find compulsory religion to their taste

side of life far more than happens in the twentieth century, though they also missed out on some of the fun and games. Preaching and organised prayer were the keynotes of the evangelical life, the preaching often being by setting a good example. They did not mind whether they were popular or not, and were willing to press for the abolition of slavery, for example, (a campaign organised by William Wilberforce, one of the earliest evangelicals), even though this might make them hated by business friends who profited from it. Study of the Bible and prayer made them sure they were right and their convictions made them unafraid.

Evangelicals in Action

Some examples of evangelicals will illustrate a few of their beliefs in action, first in education. There was no national pattern of schools in the 1820s. The government had no part in education and there was every variety of school. The public schools were as bad as most others. Great passages of Greek and Latin had to be learnt by heart. There were few teachers to the numbers of boys, and order was kept by the terror of brutal floggings. (Two companies of troops with fixed bayonets were needed to crush the boys of Winchester School in 1818 when they rebelled against such methods.)

Thomas Arnold became headmaster of Rugby in 1828 and set out to improve things at that school. He introduced French and maths to bring the curriculum up to date. He adopted the idea of making the older boys prefects and, having won their confidence, allowed them to run the school to some extent. They set a higher standard of behaviour which was followed by the younger boys. The chapel was made the centre of school life, and the whole emphasis of the school was to train people to be reliable, so that they would be the leaders in society. These new ideas in education were copied and extended by others, so that the schools became friendlier places, training the people who went into parliament and leading the country in many other ways.

One man who entered parliament, in 1826, was Ashley Cooper, later Lord Shaftesbury. He soon became the leader of attempts to improve working conditions by law. He was largely responsible for the Factory Act of 1833 which stopped young children working in cotton and worsted mills, and reduced the working hours of others. The Mines Act of 1842 was the result of his demands also. He was saddened at the amount of suffering there was in industry and in daily life. His view of religion required him to do what he could—he said in 1875, 'When I have passed away from life, I desire to have no more said of me than that I have done my duty whilst in it'. This somewhat chilly concern for others led him to take an interest in the costermongers of London, and he was chairman of the

49 (*opposite*) The Ragged School Tree clearly illustrates the evangelical background that the schools had. It also shows some of the useful off-shoots of the movement

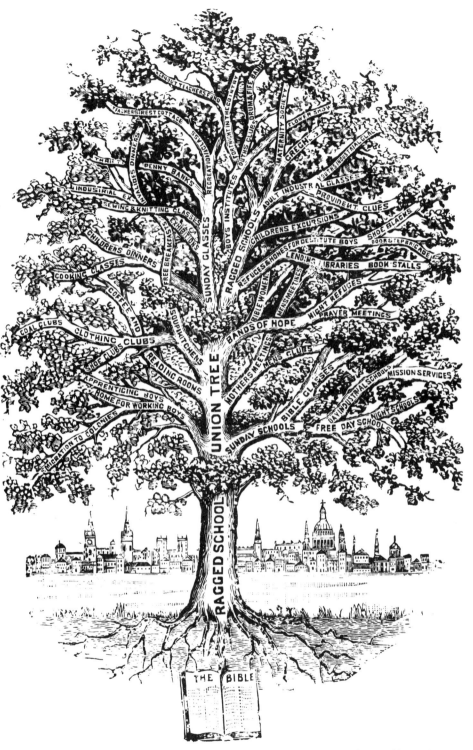

RAGGED SCHOOL TREE DRAWN BY THE LATE MR. S. E. HAYWARD.

50 The Tenby lifeboat in action in 1853. Religion did not only apply to the wealthy but stirred all kinds of people to show compassion for others in difficulties. Two centuries before, the shipwrecked would have been left to die

Ragged Schools Union for thirty-nine years. The ragged schools were run by voluntary teachers and supported by donations from the public. They offered some kind of education to the neglected children of the poorer parts of London and other towns. These, and Shaftesbury's other activities, are examples of the effects of evangelical preaching. The formation of the Royal Society for the Prevention of Cruelty to Animals in 1824 and Dr. Thomas Barnardo's home in Stepney for orphaned children are further examples from an endless list of philanthropic work sparked off by the evangelical movement.

Dissenters

The nonconformists, as the dissenters were increasingly called, did not stand aside from such activities. Many nonconformists were active in the the British and Foreign Bible Society, for example, and support for many kinds of philanthropy came from all denominations. The evangelicals of the Church of England and the nonconformists had much in common. There was the same close study of the Bible and often an unquestioning acceptance of it as fact, which was to cause difficulties later. Church attendance was as important as ever, and hard work and honesty were still admired.

The nonconformists had in other ways nothing in common with the Anglican

51 The London Cottage Mission was one of many schemes that combined religious motives with social concern

LONDON COTTAGE MISSION

Instituted in the year 1870.

Offices: 44, FINSBURY PAVEMENT, LONDON, E.C.

This Society is supported by Voluntary Contributions, and is established for the Religious, Intellectual, and Social Elevation of the Working Classes, by means of Gospel Services held in Mission Halls, &c., Cottage Meetings held in the homes of the poor or otherwise, Addresses to Tramps and others in Lodging-house Kitchens, Open Air Preaching, Special Services for Children, Sunday Schools, Mothers' Meetings, Maternity Societies, Clothing and other Clubs, Bible Classes, House to House Visitation, Tract Distribution, Lectures on Self-help, Thrift, &c., and other Social and Religious Subjects, Entertainments and Concerts, Temperance Societies, Bands of Hope, and Excursions into the Country; also

For the Benevolent and Charitable purpose of Relieving the Sick and Destitute Poor by means of Temporary or Permanent Pecuniary Aid in deserving cases, weekly Irish Stew Dinners to poor Children, and gratuitous Distribution of Food, Fuel, and Clothing.

Also supports a large Convalescent and Country Home for poor Children, with nearly One Hundred Beds, at Halls Green Farm, Sevenoaks Weald, Kent.

FUNDS ARE URGENTLY NEEDED

To develop the good work the Mission has in view. Subscriptions and Donations will be gratefully received and acknowledged by Miss F. NAPTON, the Lady Superintendent, 304, Burdett Road, Limehouse, E.; the Bankers, THE LONDON AND SOUTH-WESTERN BANK, 7, Fenchurch Street, E.C.; and by WALTER AUSTIN, *Managing Director*, 44, Finsbury Pavement, London, E.C.

church or with each other. They were firm believers in the importance of personal judgement, and every church in the Baptist, Presbyterian and Congregational churches was free to do what it thought right. They had no sense of belonging to the Church as a whole, though on the other hand they escaped the restraining hand of tradition that hindered the Anglican church at times. The members of all denominations had hard-and-fast views throughout the century, and were very intolerant of the views of others. People believed they were right and everyone else was wrong and probably wicked; they could not imagine that there was more than one way of looking at a problem, or that several people might each have part of the answer.

There were frequent and unseemly arguments within denominations. The Methodists split in 1810, for example, when the Primitive Methodists left the main body. A more serious argument in 1849–50 caused the Methodist Free Churches to go off on their own. The other denominations had no such serious splits, but were so independent as to make them a mass of separate churches under the same name. The Congregationalists (the new name for the Independents) realised that this loose connection was too vague, and formed the Congregational Union of England and Wales in 1832. Even this was a voluntary arrangement and the Union had no power over the member churches—it was hoped they would agree to co-operate with one another.

Rivalry over Education

The nonconformists quickly joined forces, however, if there was the slightest sign of a threat to their beliefs from the Anglican church, no matter how faint the threat might be. The sight of the largest churches in Britain behaving in this way was not a good example to anyone, but that did not stop them spending almost the whole century trying to gain the advantage over one another about education. Various nonconformists combined in 1808 to form the British and Foreign School Society, which was to build schools and educate children wherever there was a need. Bible-reading was to be ancouraged but religious teaching was to be undenominational. The bishops were afraid that this would undermine their church and encouraged the formation in 1811 of a similar society, whose full title indicates the purpose: 'The National Society for promoting the education of the poor in the principles of the established church'. The two societies then wasted much of their money building schools near each other, while neglecting other areas. Education continued to be the pawn of the opposing sides until the 1870s, and

52 The caption with this picture when it was published in 1872 read 'A day in the country for London children: Provided for the really deserving poor by charitable subscriptions through the National Sunday Schools Association'

53 Dinners were prepared for children in London's East End for a halfpenny each. This was in 1870

the fighting cost many rural children the chance of going to school. In 1843 a bill to cut the working day of eight-year olds from eight hours to six and a half was rejected in parliament, because nearly two million nonconformists signed petitions against provisions in the same bill that would have given the Church of England greater control over factory schools (which some employers ran within their factories). The bill became law in 1844 but nothing at all was said in it about the factory schools, which continued to be very variable as there were no regulations applicable to them. Many other examples could be mentioned of the unchristian bitterness between the churches, and a future generation was to look back on this and leave the churches alone.

The Oxford Movement

The Church of England also came under attack from within during Victorian times. This came from a group of men at Oxford University, chief of whom were John Newman and Edward Pusey. Known collectively as the Oxford movement, they tried in the 1830–40s to establish more elaborate ritual in church services.

73

They also wanted the authority of the vicars within the church to be as powerful as it used to be in the middle ages. They were very critical of all the Protestant churches, and many of the movement joined the Roman Catholic church ultimately. (John Newman became a cardinal, and also wrote *The Dream of Gerontius*.) At the time, the movement aroused the usual anti-Catholic feelings, but little support. As the century went on, more and more ritual was used in many churches. This was often unpopular with the congregations, and men in particular began to attend church less frequently.

Roman Catholics
The Roman Catholics had weathered the storm of three centuries' hatred. They had been a small and underprivileged minority at the beginning of the century. In the 1840s their numbers grew with the thousands of Irish who arrived in Liverpool looking for work. The Catholics were given the right to vote in 1829 (Catholic Emancipation Act) and could hold all but the highest offices in the government (which are still closed to them). This encouraged them, and many Catholic chapels were built. At length, the pope decided to divide the Catholics into dioceses and appoint bishops, the first since the Reformation. Immediately there was an outcry against the country being taken over by Rome. An Ecclesiastical Titles Act was rushed through parliament in 1851, making it illegal for any Catholic bishop to take the same title as an Anglican one. The Act was made mainly out of spite, for there had been no intention of duplicating titles. Catholics were increasingly accepted after the act was repealed in 1871.

Two new groups appeared in the 1820s. The Catholic Apostolic Church was founded by Edward Irving, while the Plymouth Brethren sprang up around Henry Groves and J. N. Darby. Both groups interpreted the Bible literally, were convinced that the end of the world would soon come, and were sure that there were limits to the numbers of those who would escape hell. These rather bleak beliefs were probably shared by many others outside these groups. Their narrow-minded outlook was no more narrow than many of the other churches.

Science and Religion
This narrowness left the churches no defence against new ideas—it was a long time since many church-goers had given much thought to their religion. They were not prepared for books like *Theory of the Earth* by J. Hutton (1785) or *Map of the Strata of England and Wales* by William Smith (1815). These were first attempts at geology and showed that the world was very much older than the churches understood from the Bible. *The Origin of Species* by Charles Darwin (1859) was in direct conflict with the literal story of the creation as given in the first chapters of the Bible. Churchmen of all kinds were horrified, but instead of trying to understand scientific methods, most of them attacked Darwin and his views, confident that they were right and not he. The result, spread over many years, was that the churches seemed to be clinging to out-dated notions, afraid to face new ideas

54 John Pounds was a cobbler in the mid-nineteenth century. He collected young children into his workshop and ran his own ragged school while he worked

calmly for fear that Christianity itself had been explained away. Increasing numbers of people saw nothing in such attitudes to attract them to join a church, though the decline in church-going was more of a twentieth-century situation.

Most of the nineteenth century was a church-going age, and the majority of families attended church or chapel once or twice on Sundays. There had always been a number of the poorest families in London and the other towns that the Church had never reached. They had no religious faith at all; struggling to make ends meet from one day to the next was enough to think about. William Booth tried to help such people to find a better way of life, which he was sure was only possible through religion.

Salvation Army

Booth was brought up in the 1830s, when life was grim for most people in Britain. The long wars against France had brought about many changes in daily life; much worse changes followed the war. 300,000 men were discharged from the army and navy, and expected work. They were trained only to fight, and stood little chance of being employed when more skilled men were out of work. Sweeping changes in farming and most industries had gradually abolished many unskilled jobs. Most of the tasks that had formerly been done by women and children in their homes had also been swallowed up in factories and mills. Wide-spread unemployment was further aggravated by a continuous and unprecedented rise in the population, which almost doubled between 1801 and 1851. Unemployment was not all; there was a great shortage of houses of even the worst kind, (caves were still in use in Bridgnorth, Shropshire), food was scarce and expensive, and there was no hope of any improvement in these conditions.

William Booth knew what slums were like because his father built some of them. He came into closer contact with living conditions when he was apprenticed to a pawnbroker at the age of fourteen. Men pawned their shirts to buy a drink, finding alcohol the only way out of a hopeless situation. Mothers pawned miserable belongings to pay for the next meal. Booth felt that nothing short of a revolution was needed to bring lasting improvements. He joined the Chartists for a time, who were campaigning for changes in parliament so that reforms could be made there. He soon left them, however, convinced that a religious revolution was more promising than a political one. He felt that if people put God first in their lives (and he meant all people, not just the suffering poor) living conditions would then be improved.

He needed great determination to help people to help themselves. At seventeen he began preaching to open-air meetings at street corners in Nottingham. He had to master the mockery of the crowd but he found that by talking plainly he could make people listen. He was less successful at the Wesleyan chapel of which he was a member. The Wesleyans had preached that all men were equal, and the Church had always said the same but they did not always put it into practice. In Booth's chapel, some pews were the 'best' pews for the best people, and everyone else sat further back. Booth was in trouble when he marched a column of dirty children from the streets into the best pews, although this did not daunt him. He could not understand why church people ignored the crying need for help, and could sit in their comfortable pews, uncaring. In 1849, the Wesleyans expelled him as a heretic.

During the next twelve years, Booth trained as a minister in the Reformed Methodist church, and worked as such in Halifax, Brighouse, Gateshead and Newcastle. He also married Catharine, and there were soon eight children to care for. Finally Booth resigned from the Methodist church, dissatisfied at their cosy indifference to the needs of the nation. They travelled extensively, until in desperation Catharine dragged him to London. She began preaching in Rother-

55 A Salvation Army hostel in 1892. The boxes are beds, and many women begged to be allowed to sleep on the benches when all the beds were full. Supper was provided for a penny but not all could afford even that

hithe, and made him go too. This went on every day of the week and brought complaints from 'respectable' mothers that she was abandoning her children. Many mothers had to work at this time to keep their families adequately fed and clothed—there were no widows' pensions or child allowances. Catharine's reply to criticism was to pioneer day nurseries for working mothers, where children could be cared for during the day.

William, meanwhile, tramped around the East End of London, appalled at what he saw, yet uncertain of what to do in the face of the Church's refusal to help. He still felt a religious revolution was the only answer to the problems of poverty and consequent hardship. In his travels, he came across a mission being held in a tent. He was invited to take over, and ran services at all times of the day—they did not have to be on Sundays for people who were out of work. He urged his listeners to turn to Jesus, and to give up spending their money on drink in preference to their families. This kind of talking appealed to many, but angered some who let the tent down on top of a service in 1865. Undaunted, Booth rented a dance hall, and wrote words to the popular tunes usually heard there. Gradually he began to persuade people to do as he said. He recruited helpers, often with such colourful backgrounds as Elijah Cadman, who had worked in a silk mill at the age of four, was a climbing boy from six to thirteen and a master sweep and prize fighter by seventeen. By 1869, Booth had set up his headquarters in what had been the *Eastern Star* public house in Whitechapel Road, had a weekly paper called *The War*

Cry, ran fourteen preaching stations and soup kitchens and was responsible for 140 services a week.

The organisation grew steadily, as Londoners found that these people meant it when they offered help. This was real Christianity to them. More and more helpers were recruited, and were organised on strict lines. This led 'Lijah' Cadman to call it the Salvation Army; the name was adopted in 1878 and with it much military language, brass bands and distinctive uniforms. The military side of it was not done as a dramatic gimmick, for the army was involved in a war against a variety of enemies. Whilst anyone who so wished was free to spend all their money on drink and leave their children to starve, the Army had to fight for the freedom to wear its uniform and preach in public. Brewers encouraged brawlers to break up meetings, and preachers were often the targets of stone throwing. Captain Mrs Beaty was mobbed in Hastings and died from her injuries. The authorities added persecution in the form of fines and prison sentences; three of the Booth children were gaoled in 1883, and 600 Salvationists spent some part of 1884 in prison. It was thus no stunt that preachers carried first-aid kits and that preaching stations were renamed citadels.

The Booths and the Army carried on, despite real persecution, and their courage and actions slowly changed people's views. Booth had said that all he demanded for man was 'the standard of the London cabhorse' which had 'shelter for the night, food for its stomach and work allotted to it by which it can earn its corn'. In 1890, he published a book called *In Darkest England and the Way Out*, which launched a crusade to improve living conditions. Booth still felt that a religious revolution was needed, and criticised the churches for their inadequate efforts. The crusade wanted shelters and hostels for the destitute, factories to employ them, homes for drunks and aid for discharged prisoners, labour exchanges and other reforms. Above all, Booth wanted people to trust God and transform the way they lived.

The crusade had considerable success, aided by the fact that the Salvation Army now had off-shoots all over Britain. It focussed the attention of the public on the large numbers of people living in poverty in the country, and its practical plans showed that things could change. The Army opened two labour exchanges in 1890, and had twenty-two by 1899. (The first government labour exchanges came in 1913.) It opened its own match factory and showed that they could make matches just as cheaply, but without the appalling working conditions, as the sweat shops. Public opinion forced other manufacturers to improve their conditions Many reforms were made in the years up to 1914, and many more people campaigned for them than the Salvation Army. Its contribution to improving living conditions, however, far outweighed in its variety and effect the work of others, and much of it was incorporated in the early developments of the welfare state. By that time, the Church had lost much of its influence, and many people were drifting away from it.

7   Collapse and Reconstruction

Decline in Church Attendance 1900–1914

There was a progressive decline in church attendance between 1900 and 1970. The devotion of earlier generations to Sunday worship and family prayers had begun to crumble at the end of the nineteenth century, and the crumbling became collapse in the twentieth century. The collapse released materials which could be used for rebuilding, and this chapter concerns itself with both aspects of the story. It is important to remember, however, that while there was a decline generally, many individual churches flourished and continued to be very active in helping those around them.

56   The Mission to Seamen in Whitby about 1900. The Mission provided hostels in many ports for seamen, as well as canteens and social rooms

57 The Salvation Army firewood factory at Hanbury Street, London. The army pioneered improved working conditions, and preferred to offer work rather than cash to the unemployed

Church-going did not come to an abrupt end at the turn of the century; the decline had started earlier than that and continued into the 1960s. Some of the causes of the decline were noted in the previous chapter. The increasing amount of ritual used by Anglican vicars was not popular with many people and, rather than try to change things, they stayed away from church. The narrow-minded views of most denominations, as seen in their rivalry over education, was enough to make many people think twice about whether they wished to be associated with such groups. The quality of vicars and ministers was declining before the end of the century. There were many exciting careers, such as the civil service and journalism, and new industries like electrical engineering, to appeal to those who in the past would have trained for the Church. The free churches (nonconformists) lost many potential ministers to the trade unions and the socialist movement. The Church in Britain had lost its sense of urgency and was less attractive both as a career and as a body to support. The Bible was no longer the rule-book of the upper and middle classes, and the solid core of evangelical Christians was not the powerhouse of reform and compassion it had been.

Reasons for decline could also be found outside the Church. Many more people had Saturday off by 1900, and the 'week-end' was something new. Increasing numbers of families spent it away from home, taking day-trips by train, bicycle or the spluttering charabanc. To stay for the church service took away the best part of the day so families stayed away from church. There was an increasing emphasis on pleasure, a pattern led by the Prince of Wales, which was in marked contrast to the lack of joy among the church-goers. Attempts to encourage people to enjoy themselves had incorporated the opening on Sundays of museums and galleries, from 1896. Sunday was still a holiday from work, so families could enjoy the best of both worlds—no work and no responsibility to a church. (In time,

58 A handbill produced in 1896, protesting at the proposal that any one denomination should be able to control religious instruction in the elementary schools, which educated nearly all the children. The handbill expresses the fear that the Church of England will take over the schools, and the tone of it indicates the bitterness roused over education

Why the Education Bill must be opposed.

Because it destroys the present system of undenominational teaching in Board Schools.

Clause 27 of the Bill destroys THE COWPER TEMPLE CLAUSE of the Act of 1870 which provided that in no Board School should there be any denominational teaching. Any denomination is to be allowed to teach its dogmas, if it can get hold of a "reasonable" number of parents to ask that their children may receive such instruction.

Lord Salisbury, last year, told the Church Party that what they had to do was "TO CAPTURE THE BOARD SCHOOLS." This Clause 27 is put in the Bill to enable this to be done.

The parents, whose wishes alone have to be considered in this matter of religious instruction, have never shown any dissatisfaction with the present undenominational system which has worked well for the last quarter of a century.

Not only is its destruction not asked for by the parents, but it is HIGHLY DISTASTEFUL TO THE TEACHERS, who have already strongly protested against it.

At present, though denominationalism can not be taught, religious instruction is reverently and regularly given in our Board Schools. Why should this system be destroyed to allow one particular religious body to " Capture the Schools ? "

81

Sunday became a normal working day for many and the weekend was lost again.) At this time also, increased opportunities for education, and particularly many new discoveries in science, helped to discredit the die-hard views put forward by the churches.

With so many causes of change in church attendance, it may seem surprising that the majority of people still went to church at least once on Sunday in 1900, and continued to do so at least until war began in 1914. Starting from the near-total church attendance of the 1860s, it was bound to take many years before even half the country had given up going to church regularly. Many people gave up only gradually—going to church was still 'the done thing' in the 1930s, and many families wanted to keep up appearances even if they had no positive views on religion.

The nonconformist chapels held their congregations better than the parish churches up to 1914. This was inevitable since membership of the free churches had always involved some effort; it was not the conventional church to attend. Competition came mainly from the Labour and socialist movements early in the century, which organised popular propaganda meetings on Sunday nights. In return, many conconformist churches ran meetings which were known as Pleasant Sunday Afternoons. The minister presided and there was usually a hymn and prayer but the meetings were basically non-religious. Authors, travellers and politicians gave talks which, particularly in Baptist and Congregational churches, had a marked socialist bias. Indeed, the Independent Labour Party copied most of its methods from the nonconformist churches, which may explain why it did not develop as an anti-religious party, unlike its counterparts in Europe.

The Church of England was seen to its greatest advantage in the slums of the industrial towns. Many of its best priests were at work among people who lived below the level at which self-help could do any good. One tenth of the population lived below the poverty line. For the rest, while some vicars did their work with patience and integrity, the leadership of the church as a whole was ineffective. The Anglican church retained the privileged status of being the established church. Its right to be consulted on matters of ceremony, education and morals was unquestioned and gave it considerable influence. Proposals to disestablish the Anglican church in Wales were resisted as the 'thin end of the wedge' that might force the church in England to lose its privileged status. Disestablishment was finally granted in 1914, though nothing was done until 1920 because of the war. Events soon showed that it had been a wise move to put the Anglican church on the same footing as all the other denominations in Wales. There was also much argument over proposals to revise the prayer book, and parliament was again able to exercise its control over the church. Some bishops defied parliament and allowed the new prayer book to be used in the churches in their dioceses. There was a growing shortage of candidates for training to the high standard there had been in Victoria's day, and the church lost many of its worshippers.

The turmoil beginning to be felt by all the churches did have one positive

59 A demonstration, organised against the Education Bill of 1902, brought Roman Catholics and the free churches together—nearly. The Catholics are marching behind their banner on the left, the free churches behind theirs on the right

result. They began to be more tolerant of one another's beliefs and customs. This was something that had not happened since 1500 and was long overdue. It happened particularly at the universities, where meetings of the Student Christian Movement brought together representatives of all denominations for discussion.

1914–39

The World War of 1914–18 shattered Britain in very many ways, religious no less than others. Millions of men were confronted with the sickening horror of killing and every family knew someone killed in the fighting. It was not edifying to see priests blessing guns and tanks, nor to hear both sides claiming God was on their side. This was enough to make some people sever their connections with a church. On the other hand, many individuals took a different form of action by refusing

83

60 School prayers being said at a public school. They were said in Latin

to fight. From 1915, these conscientious objectors were allowed to appear before local tribunals to put their case. 7,000 agreed to do non-combatant work and a further 3,000 were drafted into labour camps. Another 1,500 would have nothing to do with the war at all, and were court-martialled. The majority of these men objected on religious grounds, though there were also some Marxists and libertarians.

Numbers regularly going to church fell faster in the depressed years after the war. The Church did not seem able to say much that was relevant or helpful either to war-weary men or to those on the dole. The Church had partly lost the way itself, and was under attack from unexpected directions. The new sciences, particularly biology, questioned the possibility of Christ's birth and his return to life at Easter. Added to the doubts raised by Darwin's research, it hardened the conflict between science and religion. For some years between the two wars, it seemed impossible to be both a scientist and a Christian. Another attack on belief

61 The full ritual of the Church of England, seen in all its splendour at the enthronement of the hundredth Archbishop of Canterbury in 1961. Note the presence of the mayors and other dignitaries

came from the work of those who examined the early texts of the Bible, finding new meanings as a result of increased knowledge. Those who believed that the Bible was literally true felt the ground slipping away from under them.

Church attendance continued to fall, though the pattern of decline was different between the wars. The numbers of Roman Catholics remained almost constant. The Church of England had all the advantages of being established (the formally acknowledged religion of the country). Its representatives were at all official functions, its worship was used in the grammar schools and in most of the new secondary schools also, and it had twenty-six bishops in the House of Lords to put its point of view and, on occasions, defend its interests. (Nonconformists were only allowed to sit in the House of Commons; Roman Catholics were not even allowed to do that, though the atheist Charles Bradlaugh had been elected to parliament in 1880). The advantages of the Anglican church helped it to slow down the rate of loss. The free churches were the hardest hit in these years. They included many members who believed in the Bible literally and they had the bottom knocked out of their world. Many thousands of free church members saw more hope of easing the depression and ending unemployment in trade unions and socialism than they did in religion.

Political Faiths

There were two secular movements which attracted some support at this time. The more popular was the British Communist Party, which was formed from the Socialist Party in 1919. Modern communism, as worked out in London by Karl Marx, might be described as a political faith. It is based on the belief that a person's main concern in life is his own material well-being, and works toward a time when all the people in a country (ultimately the world) will co-operate to raise the living standards of everyone. No-one will then own any private property but will be entitled to share everything. There are many parallels between Communist ideas and the Christian views of the brotherhood of man; the overriding difference is that Communism denies the existence of God. It is based on the belief that self-interest is the only motive that makes someone behave as he does. The depression years and the progress of Communism in Russia encouraged some interest in it in Britain and attracted people who had seen hope of a fairer society in Christianity but grown tired of waiting.

The other group was the Fascists or Black Shirts. The British Union of Fascists was founded in 1932 by Sir Oswald Mosley. Fascism is also a political faith, which sees the state as deserving of all obedience and loyalty. The state (or the nation) is everything, and can therefore control all activities to serve its own ends. There can be no limit to the powers of the state over trade unions, employers, even family life. To question the state is treason. There is no parallel with Christianity, which is not concerned with the glories of political units. The Fascists, though few, were active in the 1930s, and there were frequent fights between groups of the two political faiths. Neither of them gained the widespread support in Britain that they did in Europe.

For all the decline in church-going, England remained Christian in morality, even if it was ceasing to believe in Christianity as a faith. The country was basically honest and standards of public duty were high. People did not clamour to be known as atheists for these were unpopular. If people became apathetic about religion in these years, the Church made few demands on them, and often those it did make were no longer relevant to modern life.

The Second World War (1939–45) had much the same effect as the First in upsetting peace-time habits. The decline in church attendance continued after the war until by the 1960s few people went to church unless they were convinced of the truth and relevance of Christianity. There are few statistics of church-going and most are unreliable for different reasons. A common estimate in the 1960s was that one person in ten regularly went to church, and that the majority of people only went for baptisms, weddings and funerals. Some churches were pulled down, others converted for homes or premises for light industry. Many more struggled on, the congregations at their wits' end for money for heating and repairs, and the preachers addressing more pews than people. The Church had, apparently, collapsed, and many forecast that it would shortly disappear completely.

Waves of Church Popularity

This had not been the first time that the Church had declined, however, and there were signs that reconstruction was under way, as at other times. If you have read this book through from the beginning, you will have noticed a continuing pattern of the Church speaking its mind boldly, becoming popular and then decaying. The Church has often been at its best only when it has been ignored or even persecuted. It is then forced to think out clearly what it believes, and only attracts members who share the beliefs and the possible mockery that goes with doing something different from most other people. At times like this, as in the tenth, twelfth and sixteenth centuries, the Methodists in the eighteenth century, the evangelicals in the 1830s and 1840s or the Salvation Army in the 1880s, sincere faiths made demands on people to believe and have courage. This has attracted others, until there was no great opposition. The Church has then grown complacent and failed to teach the new members what membership of the Church involved or to keep pace with the times.

The Church has always welcomed new members, and its services have been

62 Many churches had to be rebuilt after the Second World War. Some used the most modern architectural styles; others combined traditional stone with the latest in foam concrete to produce buildings less likely to date. This one is in Bristol

open to members and non-members alike. There could never be a rigid test of the level of a person's belief. Many people hold the beliefs (or non-beliefs) of their parents, without ever thinking them out for themselves. Language, knowledge, the way we think, the needs of people—all these are constantly changing. The Church in its popular phases has fossilised out-of-date ways and so has steered itself into a backwater. It has then become unpopular, church-going has declined and the Church has had to go back to the Bible and find again how to say what it believes, in new language and modern activities.

New Language

The Church has been involved in just such a rethinking of its beliefs in the twentieth century. As with Wyclif, for example, the thinking has been firmly based on studying the Bible and expressing it in modern English. The criticism of the Bible that was the downfall of many church-goers, referred to earlier in this chapter, was the basis of the new language for others. There has been a mass of translations and paraphrases of the Bible. It had been translated into almost every language in the world in the nineteenth century; a revision of the Authorised Version was the best that was done in English, completed in 1885. James Moffat made a translation of the New Testament in 1913 and completed the whole Bible in 1926. The most recent of the translations has been the New English Bible, which has replaced the Authorised Version in many churches. In addition, many attempts have been made to express the Bible in everyday language, such as the books by J. B. Phillips in the 1950s.

The shake-up in the way the Church talks has also been seen in hymns, both words and tunes. Geoffrey Beaumont's lively tune for *Now Thank We All Our God* is widely used, for example, and has largely replaced the older and more pompous tune. One example of modern words is this by Richard Jones:

> God of concrete, God of steel,
> God of piston and of wheel,
> God of pylon, God of steam,
> God of girder and of beam,
> God of atom, God of mine,
> All the world of power is thine.

There are three more verses to this, and many more examples of new hymns and religious songs.

Ecumenical Movement

Renewed life in the Church has been seen in other ways too. One has been a certainty that the Church has not been active enough in telling non-Christians about Christ and attempts to improve matters. An early attempt was the World Missionary Conference held in Edinburgh in 1910. Representatives from many

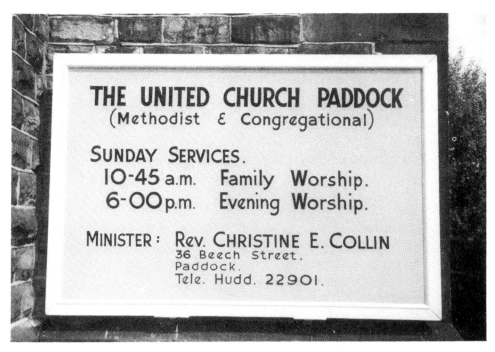

63 An example of a local union between neighbouring churches. Shortly after this photograph was taken, the church became part of the United Reformed Church

parts of the world and most of the large denominations took part, and resolved to keep in touch in order to improve the Church's missionary work in the world.

The members of the conference realised that one of the main stumbling blocks to telling other people about Christ was the maze of divisions which split the Church into fragments. The sight of three or four churches in the same street, all different, was enough to make any thinking person wonder which, if any, was the right one. Parts of hymns, such as 'We are not divided, all one body we', were made meaningless. It therefore dawned on many Christians that the churches must seek to unite into one again. (It is important to distinguish between unity and uniformity.) The movement towards this goal has become known as the ecumenical movement. Conferences have been held in many parts of the world, each one attended by a wider variety of denominations and nationalities. The conferences culminated in the formation of the World Council of Churches at Amsterdam in 1948, a body representative of more nationalities than the United Nations.

This fact makes it a little meaningless to talk of the ecumenical movement in Britain on its own, for the Church has always been an international body. At the more local level, there was a growing sense of co-operation among different denominations, especially after 1950. Many churches set out to learn more about

89

both themselves and their neighbours, and in so doing frequently found that they agreed on more things than they disagreed on. There have already been some local unions of neighbouring churches, mainly among the free churches, who were impatient of the divisions in the Church. The Methodist and Anglican churches have been discussing re-uniting for a number of years, while the Presbyterian and Congregational churches amalgamated to form the United Reformed church in 1972. This was the first major reunion since the divisions began at the reformation. Many churches attended a conference at Nottingham in 1968 and resolved to unite by 1980. Time will tell.

In these ways, the Church has been reconstructing itself to show its relevance to the twentieth century. The Church in Britain is becoming aware of its place in the world Church, and is recovering its self-confidence. It is nearly ready for the next stage of fearless expression of its beliefs, to people who are either hostile or apathetic to Christianity but who yet seek a satisfying religion.

Reconstruction is by no means the only matter that concerns the present-day Church. The old idea of serving the needs of people is still met. This may be in organising youth clubs or meetings for the elderly, or in allowing groups such as the Scouts, pre-school play groups or the Samaritans the use of buildings. Many individual Christians are active within such bodies, and the influence of the Church is greater than its numbers might suggest. Increasingly the contribution of the Church to society is being made in these unobtrusive ways, instead of attempting to lay down the law. The Church has been most effective in the past when it has been offering something to society rather than demanding something from it.

8 Today, Tomorrow

'We all seem to have a natural desire to worship something greater than ourselves.' Each generation and every individual decides for itself its view of religion. Roman emperors, Thor and Woden, the dark shadows of witchcraft and Christ have all been the focus of attention for people in Britain in the past two thousand years. Of these, Christianity has offered a satisfying religion to more people, though often marred by the Church's own shortcomings.

64 The Roman Catholic Cathedral in Liverpool, completed in 1967, is an example of the use of new materials to make a style of building that lends itself to the services now being developed

65 An evangelical singing group in the 1970s, photographed together with some children. Their joyful enthusiasm is self-evident

At the present time, there is much doubt about the value of Christianity in a space age. This does not mean that people are irreligious (though some are), but that they are questioning the beliefs accepted by previous generations. Renewed interest in witchcraft and black magic on the one hand, and the excitement aroused by the Beatles' interest in eastern mystics is proof enough that many people feel the existence of an outside force influencing their lives. They will seek an explanation for this.

Nearly all the world's religions are represented in Britain now, giving British people a unique opportunity to study the beliefs and practices of those who have tried to explain religious mysteries. There are one and a half million Muslims in Britain, most of whom have come from Pakistan and Bangladesh. Perhaps a million Hindus have come from India, and there are also a number of Sikhs.

About half a million Jews live in Britain, and there are small communities of many other religions.

There has never been a time when it has been so easy to find out the beliefs of the main religions. It is clear that religion plays a very important part in a person's life, guiding his behaviour and attitude to others. The lack of religious convictions is also a strong influence, leaving people without any goal to steer towards. This may be in part the cause behind the outbreaks of violence at the present time, and the high levels of dishonesty, waste and lack of consideration for other people's feelings. An irreligious person does not have to be an unpleasant member of society any more than church attendance makes a man a saint; the fact remains that people with some religious views are more likely to behave with some thought for others than not.

It may be appropriate to end this chapter with a modern psalm by a teenager:

> Who is God?
>   What is God?
> Is He really true?
>   Does He work wonders?
> I wish I knew.
>
> Is He in the green trees?
>   Is He in the meadow?
> 'Is He in the latest beat,
>   Is He in the twisting feet?
> Is He real?
>   Is He true?
> Oh! I say! I wish I knew!

Further Reading

The subject of religious history is so wide and the range of books available so great that the following list is intended only to suggest the kind of books that may prove helpful.

The best way to find out what churches and monasteries were like as buildings is to go and see them. The maps published by the Ordnance Survey of *Roman Britain, Britain in the Dark Ages* and *Monastic Britain* are a guide to sites in your own area. K. A. Lindley, *How to Explore: Abbeys and Monasteries* (ESA, 1961) will help you make the most of your visits. Many churches are still in use after many centuries, and often have a short history or guide available. Ruined monasteries in the care of the Department for the Environment also have historical guides.

Books that will add further details include A. Weighall, *Wanderings in Anglo-Saxon Britain;* H. Trevor-Roper, *The Rise of Christian Europe* (Thames & Hudson, 1965); C. Petrie, *Great Beginnings* (Macmillan, 1967) and M. Hussey, *Chaucer's World* (CUP, 1967). Most denominations have their own printed histories, for example A. Peel, *A Brief History of English Congregationalism* (Independent Press, 1960).

Biographies abound, and books like D. Attwater, *The Penguin Dictionary of Saints* (1965) and D. Northcroft, *Great Women Pioneers* (Epworth Press, 1964) contain useful facts. P. Caraman, *Henry Morse, Priest of the Plague* (Fontana, 1962), G. Fry, *Richard Baxter, Toleration and Tyranny* (Longmans, 1961) and E. Bishop, *Blood and Fire, the Story of William Booth* (Longmans, 1964) give a variety of insights into problems of their times. S. Neill, *Men of Unity* (SCM, Press, 1960) illustrates the growth of the ecumenical movement.

There are many local books, which must be sought in libraries and from local publishers. Examples about the middle ages include A. M. Wilkinson, *Ripon Five Hundred Years Ago* and *The Fountains Story*. W. Edwards, *Redland Park Congregational Church* (1941) throws light on the Church's concern about living conditions in the past hundred years.

Books on other religions are making their way into school libraries. Examples are J. B. Taylor, *Thinking about Islam*; M. Domnitz, *Thinking about Judaism* (Lutterworth, 1971) and P. Bridger, *A Hindu Family in Britain* (Religious Education Press, 1969).

There are very many helpful books available. The best thing to do is decide exactly what it is you want to know and then ask a librarian. It will not help you much just to ask for a book on the history of religion—there are too many.

Index

Numbers in **bold type** refer to the figure numbers of the illustrations.